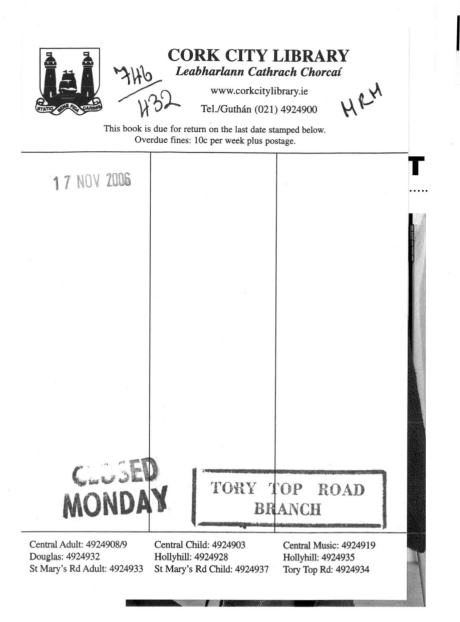

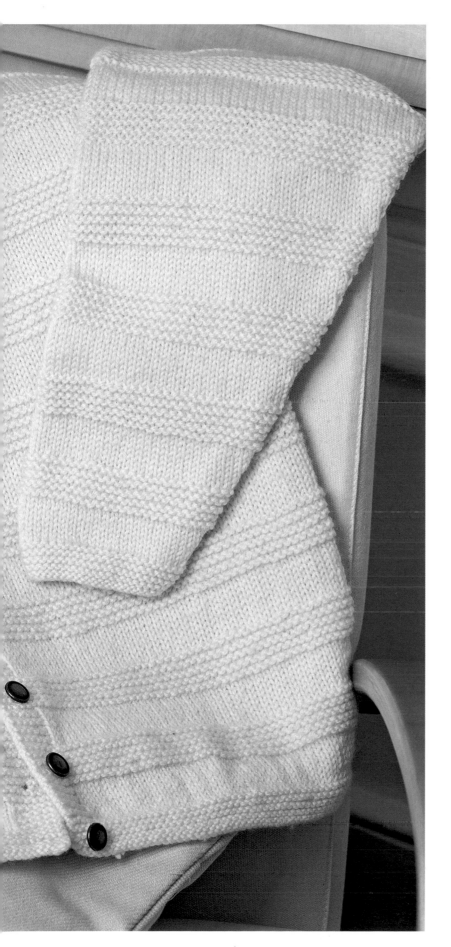

LEARN TO KNIT

....

PENNY HILL

NEW
HOLLAND

First published in 2003 by
New Holland Publishers (UK) Ltd
London · Cape Town · Sydney · Auckland

Garfield House, 86–88 Edgware Road
London W2 2EA
United Kingdom
www.newhollandpublishers.com

80 McKenzie Street
Cape Town 8001
South Africa

Level 1, Unit 4, 14 Aquatic Drive
Frenchs Forest, NSW 2086
Australia

218 Lake Road
Northcote, Auckland
New Zealand

ISBN 1 84330 842 8

Senior Editor: Clare Sayer
Production: Hazel Kirkman
Design: Frances de Rees
Photographer: Shona Wood
Editorial Direction: Rosemary Wilkinson

3 5 7 9 10 8 6 4 2

Reproduction by Pica Digital PTE Ltd, Singapore
Printed and bound by Times Offset (M) Sdn. Bhd., Malaysia

CONTENTS

INTRODUCTION

Most people lead a very hectic life, and knitting can be used as a good antidote to the stresses of that kind of lifestyle. It is calming, rewarding and can become very addictive. It can also be done by anybody – politicians and actors hit the headlines when they do it.

If you have never knitted before, now is a good time to start. There is a large selection of yarns available in a good range of classic colours as well as more fashionable and modern ones. Go to a knitting department in any large store and feel the enthusiasm from customers while choosing their yarns. Sales staff are there to help with any queries you may have.

It is possible to teach yourself to knit with a little practice and some patience. Following the techniques shown in this book, you could become expert in no time. You can knit by yourself on the bus or train and even in front of the television. Get together with some friends for a social evening and knit together – it is a great opportunity to swap patterns and exchange ideas about how to use knitting to create clothes, accessories and things for the home.

Sadly, knitting is no longer a skill that is passed from generation to generation. Perhaps you could use it as an opportunity to ask for help from your mother or grandmother – I am sure they will be surprised at your interest in this "dying" art. Remember to pass on the skill to your sons and daughters and keep the art alive.

Penny Hill.

Basic Information

Yarn comes in various thicknesses and types and a whole range of needles and gadgets are available. The following information will help you decide what you will need.

YARNS

Yarn is divided into two main types – natural and synthetic. Natural yarn is more expensive, but is more pleasant to wear and easier to handle when knitting. Synthetic yarn is cheaper and stronger and also lasts longer.

Natural yarns

Wool is easily available, long lasting and very warm, and comes from sheep which are bred for their fleeces. Merino sheep have the most abundant and highest quality yarn.

Mohair yarn comes from goats which originated in Turkey. The long brushed fibres are extremely thick and warm.

Angora is an expensive, soft and warm yarn which comes from the short-haired albino rabbit of the same name.

Cashmere is the most expensive and luxurious of yarns. Spun with a high percentage of wool, it comes from a special breed of goat.

Alpaca is a soft, high-quality fibre with a slight hairiness which comes from a species of camel related to the llama.

Silk knitting yarns are heavy and therefore expensive, but mixed with other fibres produce a strong, durable thread.

Cotton is a strong, non-allergenic, easy-to-wash yarn that has little elasticity.

Synthetic yarns

Man-made yarns have improved dramatically over the last few years — they are no longer lifeless with little elasticity. Clever combinations of synthetic and natural fibres produce fashionable, strong and lightweight yarns, the cost of which compares favourably with more expensive natural fibres.

Lurex is a shining metallic yarn available in many colours or may be a single thread used as one of the plys when the yarn is spun.

Yarn thickness

Yarn is formed by twisting together a number of strands, or plys, of fibre. Double knitting, 3-ply, 4-ply, Aran and Chunky are only general descriptions as plys can vary in thickness, so great care has to be taken when substituting yarns.

BELOW, from top to bottom: wool, mohair, angora, tweed effect yarn, silk, cotton, lurex mix.

Yarn texture

During the spinning process, fibres can be fused together at different rates.

Bouclé is produced by introducing one ply at a faster rate than the other two, so that it buckles up.

Mohair is a brushed loop yarn, with a fluffy appearance.

Slub yarns have at least one ply that varies in thickness, producing an uneven look.

Tweed effects are formed by adding coloured blips to longer fibres.

EQUIPMENT

All that is needed to produce a piece of knitted fabric is a pair of knitting needles, although you may find some basic essentials rather useful.

Needles

Needles are available in plastic, wood, bamboo, steel or alloy. Whichever type you choose, it should make no difference to the tension or quality of your work. It is all a matter of personal choice.

Pairs of needles These range in size from 0 to 15 (US), or 2 mm to 10 mm (metric), and come in three lengths: 25 cm (10 in), 30 cm (12 in) and 35 cm (14 in). Use the length which you find most comfortable for the number of stitches you are working with and the type of pattern you are knitting.

Circular needles are used for knitting tubular, seamless fabrics or for knitting flat rounds. They consist of two short needles

ABOVE, from top to bottom: bouclé, mohair, ribbon yarn, tweed.

joined by a length of nylon which varies in length. They can also be used as a pair of needles, working backwards and forwards, for patterns with a large number of stitches. Always store the needles in their original packet as they do not have their size stamped on them.

Double-pointed needles are available in sets of four or six. They are often used to knit neckbands and can be used as an alternative to circular needles where a pattern has a small number of stitches which may be too stretched on a circular needle. Double-pointed needles are used for seamless socks, gloves and berets.

Cable needles are short straight needles (or they may have a U-bend), available in 3 sizes. They are used for moving stitches from one

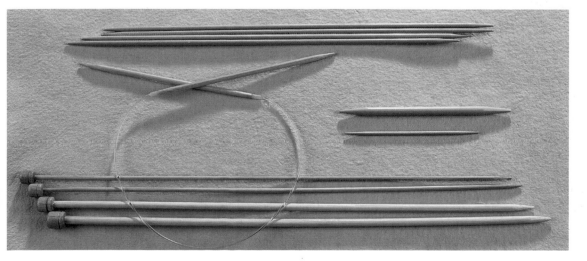

LEFT, clockwise from top: double-pointed needles, cable needles, pairs of needles, circular needles.

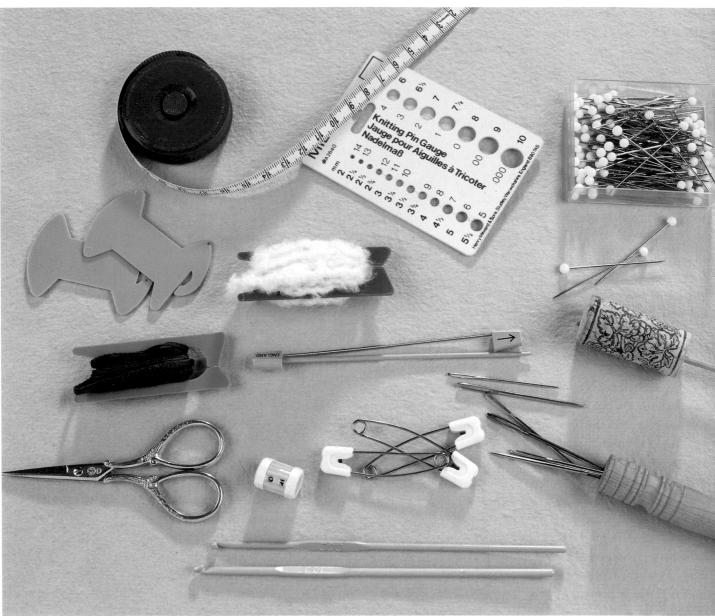

position to another when working cables. Use the needle size which corresponds to the type of yarn and main needles.

Other basics

Stitch-holders are useful for "holding" a small amount of stitches until they are needed.

Safety pins can be used instead of a stitch-holder for 4 or 5 stitches.

Tape measure Choose a strong measure that cannot stretch as this can distort your measurements. Always use either inches or centimetres.

Scissors can be small but must be sharp, as some yarns are very strong and cannot be easily broken.

Pins can disappear in the knitting if they are too small, so choose long ones with coloured glass or plastic heads.

Sewing needles with large eyes and blunt ends are used for sewing up items as sharp needles can split the yarn and weaken it.

Needle gauge Useful for checking the sizes of circular and double-pointed needles which do not have the size stamped on them.

Row counter Useful for keeping track of rows worked, particularly when increasing and decreasing.

Yarn bobbins are used for holding small

ABOVE, top row, from left to right: tape measure, needle gauge, pins; middle row, from left to right: yarn bobbins, stitch holder, cork; bottom row, from left to right: scissors, row counter, crochet hooks, safety pins, needles.

amounts of yarn, wound from the main ball, when working colour patterns.

Crochet hooks A small, medium and large size are useful for picking up dropped stitches and working edgings on finished garments.

Corks are used to put on the end of knitting needles to prevent stitches from falling off and to make them safer when not in use.

CLEANING AND STORING

It is best to clean hand-knitted garments lightly and often, but with great care. Hand-knits are not as resilient as ready-made garments – they are more likely to stretch out of shape or shrink if not handled carefully. Unless the ball band specifically states that the yarn can be machine washed, it is safest to hand wash or dry clean.

Hand washing

Use a special powder or solution for hand washing delicate fabrics. Completely dissolve the washing agent in warm water, then add sufficient cold water to make it lukewarm.

Immerse the garment in the suds and work quickly, using your hands to expel soapy water by gentle squeezing, never wringing.

Carefully lift the garment out of the water, supporting it with both hands. Rinse the garment in clear water of the same temperature until the water runs clear. After rinsing, squeeze out as much water as possible, but do not wring.

Drying

Drying needs as much care as washing. Supporting the weight of the garment, transfer it to a colourfast towel and lay it flat. Roll up the towel loosely so that excess moisture is transferred to the towel.

Lightly shake the garment to even out the stitches, lay it on a fresh dry towel and gently reshape it back to its original size. Leave the garment to dry naturally until all the excess moisture has been absorbed by the towel.

Natural fibres may be spun dry on a short gentle cycle. It is recommended that cotton is spun as retained moisture may distort the garment.

Storage

Again, correct storage is as important as washing and drying. Never hang a knitted garment up, as the weight of the garment pulls it out of shape and the ends of the hanger can distort the shape of shoulders.

Folding a garment

1. Lay the garment on a flat surface with both sleeves fully extended.
2. Fold in one sleeve diagonally in line with the side of the garment.
3. Double the sleeve back on itself to form a straight edge with the side of the garment.
4. Repeat steps 2 and 3 for the other side.
5. Fold the garment in half and store.

If the garment is to be stored for a long time, interleave tissue paper in the folds and place the garment in a plastic bag with plenty of holes in it before storing.

In the Beginning...

Before casting on, practise holding the needles and yarn – this is important as it controls the tension of the fabric. There are several ways of casting on and knitting, including continental methods – use whichever feels most comfortable for you.

HOLDING THE YARN

1. Holding the yarn in the left hand, pass it under and around the little finger of the right hand, then take it over the third finger, under the second finger and over the index finger. The index finger is used to wind the yarn round the tip of the needle. The yarn wound round the little finger controls the tension of the yarn.

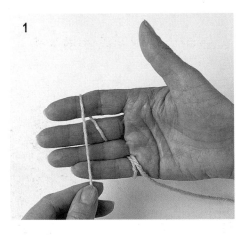

HOLDING THE NEEDLES

1. Hold the right needle in the same position as you would hold a pencil. When casting on and for the first few rows, the knitting passes easily between the thumb and index finger. As the knitting grows larger, place the thumb underneath the knitting, holding the needle from below.

Hold the left needle lightly over the top, using the thumb and index finger to control the tip of the needle.

CASTING ON — CABLE METHOD

This method of casting on gives a neat firm edge with a cable appearance.

1. Leaving enough yarn for sewing up the seam, make a slip knot and place it on the left-hand needle.

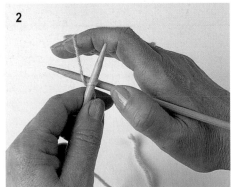

2. Holding the yarn at the back of the needles, insert the tip of the right-hand needle into the slip knot, and pass the yarn over the tip of the right-hand needle.

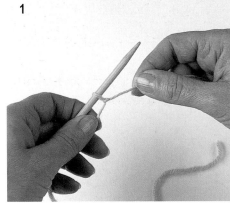

3. Draw the right-hand needle and the yarn back through the slip knot, forming a loop on the right-hand needle. Leave the slip knot on the left-hand needle.

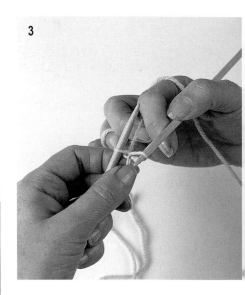

4. Transfer the new loop on to the left-hand needle. There are now two stitches on the left-hand needle.

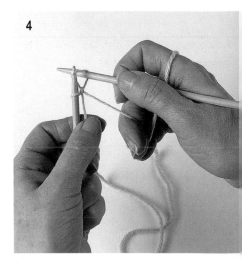

5. Insert the right-hand needle between the two stitches on the left-hand needle, and wind the yarn round the tip of the right-hand needle.

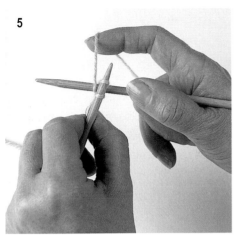

6. Draw a loop through again and place it on the left-hand needle.

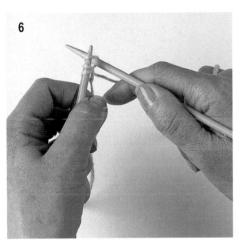

7. Repeat steps 5 and 6 until you have the required number of stitches.

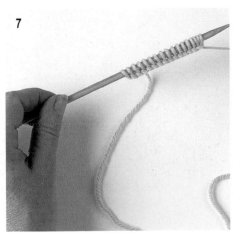

BASIC STITCHES
How to knit

The knit stitch is the most important stitch in knitting as it forms the basis for all knitted fabrics.

1. Hold the needle with the cast-on stitches in your left hand. With the yarn at the back, insert the right-hand needle from front to back through the first stitch on the left-hand needle.

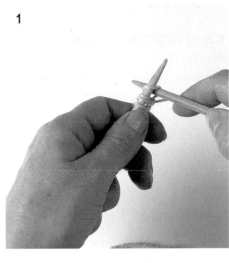

2. Wind the yarn from left to right over the tip of the right-hand needle.

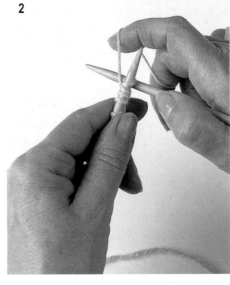

3. Draw the yarn through the stitch on the left-hand needle, making a new stitch on the right-hand needle.

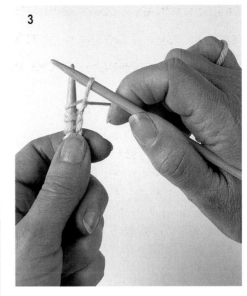

4. Slip the original stitch off the left-hand needle.

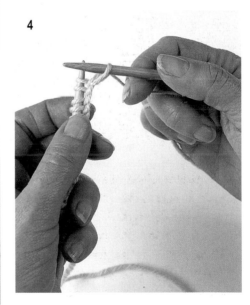

5. To knit a row, repeat steps 1 to 4 until all the stitches have been transferred from the left-hand needle to the right-hand needle. Turn the work and transfer the needle with the stitches on to the left hand to work the next row.

How to cast off

Casting off should be done in the same stitch and at the same tension as the knitting — if it is too tight, the knitting will pucker. Try using a larger needle if you have problems.

1. Knit the first two stitches in the usual way, so both the stitches are on the right-hand needle.

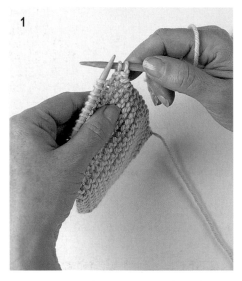

2. Use the tip of the left-hand needle to lift the first knitted stitch.

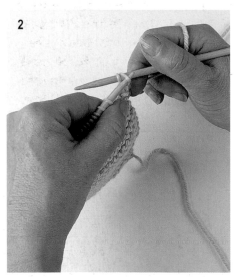

3. Pass this stitch over the second stitch and off the needle.

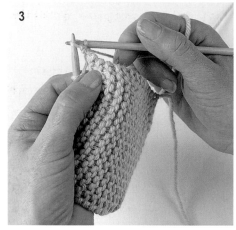

4. Knit another stitch on to the right-hand needle, and repeat from step 2 until one stitch remains. Lengthen the stitch and take it off the needle. Leaving a long length of yarn for seaming, pull the end of the yarn through the final stitch to tighten it.

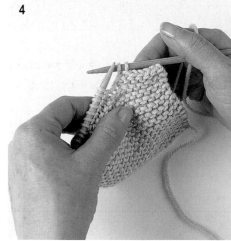

Left-handed knitters

Following the instructions for casting on, prop the book in front of a mirror and follow the diagrams in the mirror image. The yarn will then be controlled by the left hand.

Knitting by the continental method may be the solution, as you are working in the same direction as a right-handed knitter, but holding the yarn in the left hand.

How to cast on – German thumb and finger method

This is a quick way of casting on using one needle. It is suitable for yarns with little elasticity, such as cottons.

Measure out approximately 2 cm (1 in) of yarn for every stitch to be cast on. Make a slip knot at this point and slip it on the needle.

1. Wrap the ball end of the yarn around the left index finger and the cut end of the yarn around the left thumb. Wrap both ends of the yarn around the little finger.

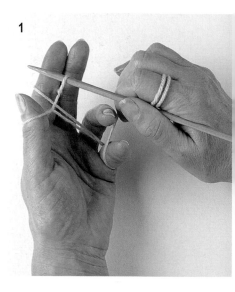

2. With the needle in the right hand, insert the tip of the needle upwards through the loop on the thumb and downwards through the loop on the index finger.

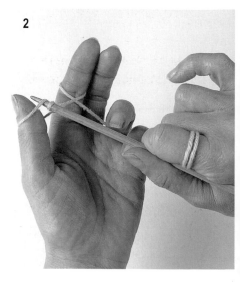

3. Draw the loop back through the loop on the thumb, then remove the thumb from the loop.

3

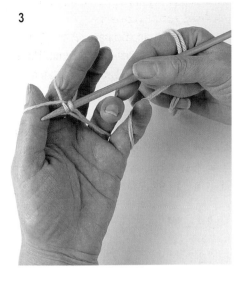

4. Use the thumb to pull the loop tight to form a new stitch.

4

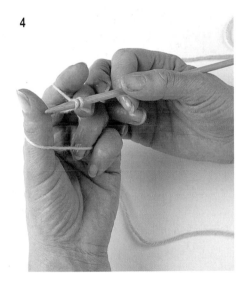

5. Repeat steps 1 to 4 until you have the required number of stitches on the needle.

How to knit – continental style

This method of knitting is often used by left-handed knitters, as the yarn is controlled by the left hand.

1. Hold the yarn in your left hand with it looped round the index finger. Insert the right-hand needle from front to back into the stitch to be knitted, then twist it under the working strand of yarn from the index finger.

1

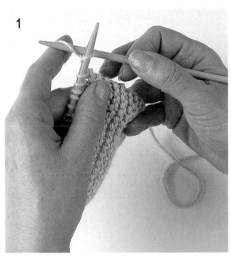

2. Use the right-hand needle to draw a new stitch through, then drop the loop from the left-hand needle.

2

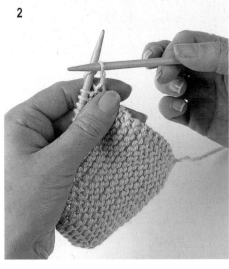

JOINING IN A NEW BALL OF YARN

Unless an enormous ball of yarn is used, it will be necessary at some time or other to join in a new ball of yarn.

1. Leaving enough yarn to darn in, and using a simple knot, join the new yarn to the long end remaining from the old ball.

1

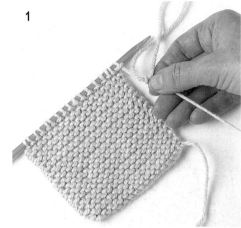

2. Slip this knot up close to the work before working the first stitch of the row.

SIMPLE SEAMS

Garter stitch lends itself to being oversewn. The row ends form little blips which can be matched one for one and joined together. Thread the needle through the bottom of the stitch on one side and the top of the corresponding stitch on the other side. This produces a flat seam which does not interrupt the lines of garter stitch.

Following a Pattern

Most knitting patterns are produced by yarn manufacturers or appear in magazines. They give you all the information you need to produce a garment that looks like the illustration. The information is usually presented in a logical form that is easy to follow.

MATERIALS

This is usually the first paragraph that appears on the pattern. It tells you how much yarn you need, what size needles to use and whether you need cable needles or buttons, etc.

MEASUREMENTS

Measurements are very important as they tell you what the finished size of the garment will be. Compare the "actual measurements" with the "to fit" measurements, as the amount of ease given can vary from style to style. You may want to make a size smaller or larger than the size to fit you, if you do not feel happy with the amount of room in the garment. Once you have decided which size is for you, go through the pattern and mark your size so that it is easy to read.

TENSION

Tension is the most important part of producing a perfect garment. The tension stated in the pattern is the one obtained by the designer, using the quoted yarn and needle size, and therefore used to design the garment and produce the stated measurements.

MAKING AND MEASURING A TENSION SWATCH

Make a sample swatch, using the yarn and needles stated in the pattern. The tension is usually given over 10 cm (4 in), but you will need to make a swatch at least 15 cm (6 in) square. Place the sample on a padded surface and gently smooth it into shape without distorting the stitches. Pin the corners and sides as shown, unrolling the edges if necessary and inserting the pins at right angles to the fabric.

To find out the stitch tension, use pins as markers and count the number of stitches

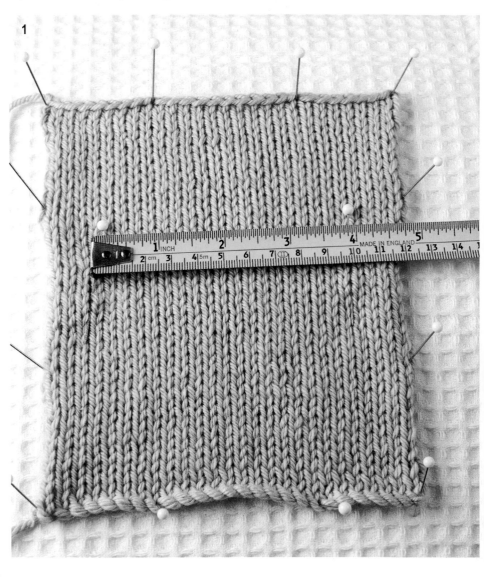

1

recommended in the tension given in the instructions. Using a rigid ruler, measure the distance between the pins. If your tension is correct it should measure 10 cm (4 in). If you have fewer stitches than stated it means your knitting is too loose; if you have more stitches than stated your knitting is too tight. If your tension is too loose make another swatch using smaller needles. If your tension is too tight make another swatch using larger

needles. Your tension must be accurate, if it is only one stitch out, it could make the finished garment too big or too small.

For the row tension follow the same procedure as for the stitch tension. On stocking stitch, it may be easier to work from the back as each ridge is one row. If your stitch tension is accurate but your row tension is slightly out, this should not make much difference to most garments.

ABBREVIATIONS

Abbreviations are used in knitting patterns to keep the instructions short and precise. If every work was written in long hand, it would be like reading a book. The following abbreviations are the ones most commonly used:

alt	alternate
beg	beginning
cm	centimetres
cont	continue
dec	decreas(e)(ing)
foll	following
gst	garter st, every row k
in	inches
inc	increas(e)(ing)
k	knit
m1	make 1 st by picking up the bar between the st just worked and the next st on the left-hand needle and working into the back of it
mm	millimetres
p	purl
patt	pattern
rem	remain(ing)
rep	repeat
RS	right side
sl	slip
skpo	slip 1, knit 1, pass slipped st over
st(s)	stitch(es)
st st	stocking stitch, k on right side and p back
tbl	through back of loop
tog	together
WS	wrong side
ytf	yarn to front
yf	yarn forward to make one st

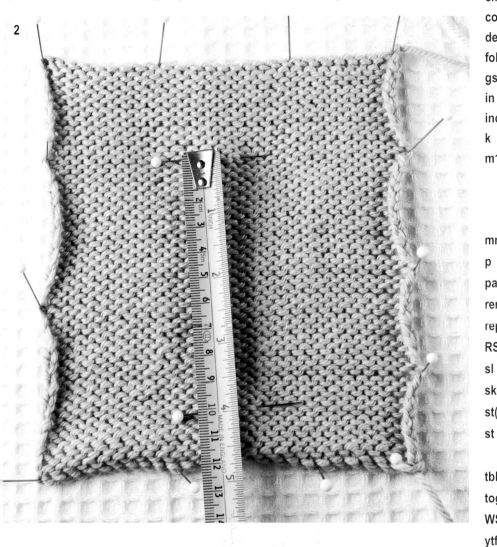

2

WRITTEN INSTRUCTIONS

These are the main part of the pattern and tell you how to make a garment from beginning to end. The instructions are given headings which are usually in a bold type so they are easily spotted when reading the instructions. An asterisk (*) is a common symbol in knitting instructions, it is used to save the same instruction being used over and over

again, for example, * p1, k1; rep from * to end of row, means you just keep working p1, k1, until the last stitch has been knitted. Another space-saving technique is to put instructions that are to be repeated in square brackets ([ ]) and then state how many times they are to be repeated, for example, [p1, k1] 4 times.

Baby Hat and Scarf

Garter stitch produces a reversible fabric which makes it ideal for scarves and hats with brims. To make this hat and scarf all you need to know is how to cast on, knit and cast off.

MEASUREMENTS

To fit age   0-3 months

MATERIALS

For the set

3 x 50 g balls of Debbie Bliss wool/cotton in pale lilac or pale blue

Pair of 3¾ mm (US 5) knitting needles

TENSION

25 stitches and 46 rows to 10 cm (4 in) square measured over garter stitch using 3¾ mm (US 5) needles.

SCARF

With 3¾ mm (US 5) needles, cast on 30 stitches.

Work in garter stitch (every row knit) until scarf measures 60 cm (23½ in) from cast-on edge.

Cast off.

HAT

With 3¾ mm (US 5) needles, cast on 51 stitches.

Continue in garter stitch (every row knit) until hat measures 36 cm (14 in) from cast-on edge.

Cast off.

To Make Up

Fold hat in half and join the two side seams. Fold brim to right side.

Basic Fabrics

All knitted fabrics are made using just two basic stitches – knit and purl.

Garter stitch is often referred to as plain knitting because every row is knitted or purled. This produces a reversible fabric with raised horizontal ridges on both sides of the work. It is looser than stocking stitch. One of the advantages of garter stitch is that it does not curl, so it can be used on its own or for bands and borders.

Stocking stitch is the most widely used knitted fabric. With the knit side as the right side it makes a flat, smooth surface that tends to curl at the edges. It needs finishing with bands, borders or hems where there would otherwise be a raw edge.

Reversed stocking stitch is the "wrong side" of stocking stitch and can be used in the same way as stocking stitch. It is similar in appearance to garter stitch but gives a closer, flatter fabric.

HOW TO PURL

Once you have mastered the art of knit stitch, the next step is how to purl.

1. Hold the needle with the stitches on in your left hand. With the yarn at the front of the work, insert the right-hand needle through the front of the first stitch on the left-hand needle.

1

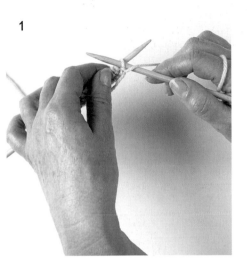

2. Wind the yarn from right to left over the tip of the right-hand needle.

2

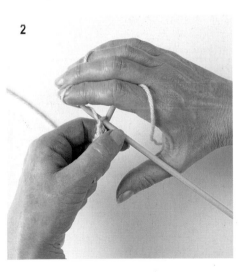

3. Draw the yarn through the stitch on the left-hand needle, making a new stitch on the right-hand needle.

3

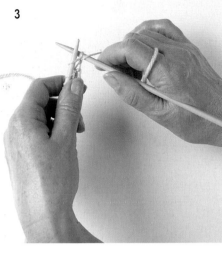

4. Slip the original stitch off the left-hand needle.

4

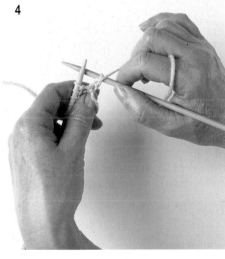

5. To purl a row, repeat steps 1 to 4 until all the stitches have been transferred from the left-hand needle to the right-hand needle. Turn the work and transfer the needle with the stitches on to the left hand to work the next row.

How to purl — continental style

1. Holding the yarn in your left hand and keeping your index finger to the right of where you are working, insert the right-hand needle from back to front through the stitch to be purled.

1

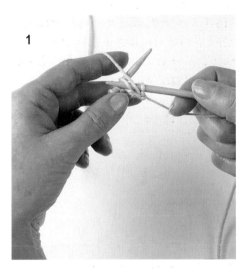

2. Bring the working yarn forward slightly, then twist the right-hand needle from left to right around the yarn. Draw a new stitch through and drop the original stitch from the left-hand needle.

2

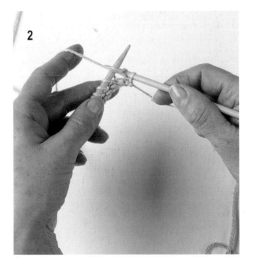

Three Cushions

To make these cushions all you need to know is how to cast on, knit, purl and cast off.

GARTER STITCH CUSHION

MEASUREMENTS

32 x 32 cm (12½ x 12½ in)

MATERIALS

4 x 50 g balls of Jaeger Merino Aran in dark grey
Pair of 4½ mm (US 7) knitting needles
Cushion pad, 35 x 35 cm (14 x 14 in)

TENSION

19 stitches and 42 rows to 10 cm (4 in) square measured over garter stitch using 4½ mm (US 7) needles.

Back

Cast on 61 stitches.
1st row: Knit to end.
This row forms the garter stitch pattern.
Continue in garter stitch until work measures 32 cm (12½ in) from cast-on edge.
Cast off.

Front

Work exactly the same as for the Back.

To Make Up

Sew the two cast-on edges together, then join the two pairs of side edges. Insert cushion pad and join remaining seam to finish.

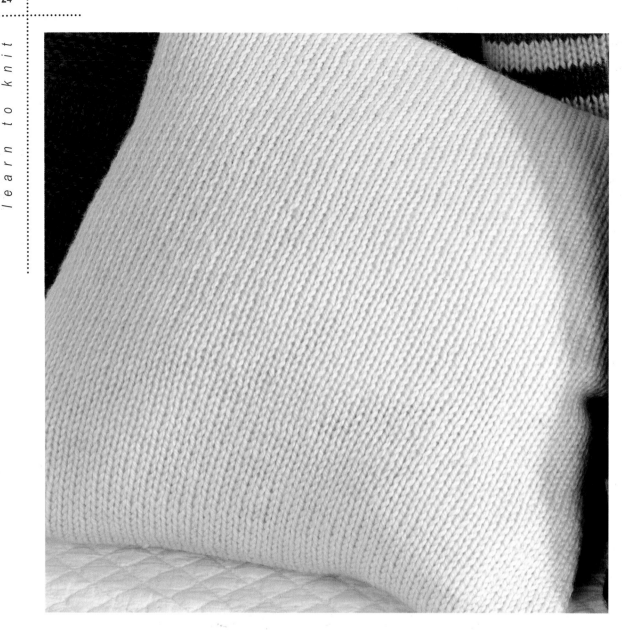

STOCKING STITCH CUSHION

MEASUREMENTS

33 x 33 cm (13 x 13 in)

MATERIALS

3 x 50 g balls of Jaeger Merino Aran in cream
Pair of 4½ mm (US 7) knitting needles
Cushion pad, 35 x 35 cm (14 x 14 in)

TENSION

19 stitches and 25 rows to 10 cm (4 in) square measured over stocking stitch using 4½ mm (US 7) needles.

Back

Cast on 63 stitches.
1st row: Knit to end.
2nd row: Purl to end.
These two rows form the stocking stitch pattern.
Continue in stocking stitch until work measures 33 cm (13 in) from cast-on edge. Cast off.

Front

Work exactly the same as for the Back.

To Make Up

Sew the two cast-on edges together, then join the two pairs of side edges. Insert cushion pad and join remaining seam to fnish.

STOCKING STITCH AND GARTER STITCH CUSHION

MEASUREMENTS

32 x 32 cm (12½ x 12½ in)

MATERIALS

3 x 50 g balls of Jaeger Merino Aran in grey
Pair of 4½ mm (US 7) knitting needles
Cushion pad, 35 x 35 cm (14 x 14 in)

TENSION

19 stitches and 25 rows to 10 cm (4 in) square measured over stocking stitch using 4½ mm (US 7) needles.

Back

Cast on 61 stitches.
Knit 9 rows.
Next row: Knit to end.
Next row: **Purl to end.**
Repeat the last 2 rows three times more.
Knit 10 rows.
The last 18 rows form the pattern of stripes of stocking stitch and garter stitch.
Continue in pattern until work measures 32 cm (12½ in) from cast-on edge, ending with 10 rows garter stitch.
Cast off.

Front

Work exactly the same as for the Back.

To Make Up

Sew the two cast-on edges together, then join the two pairs of side edges. Insert cushion pad and join remaining seam to finish.

Textured Stitches

Simple textured stitches are formed by working knit and purl stitches in the same row.

Moss stitch is a basic textured stitch. It is made up of alternating knit and purl stitches. Stitches that are knitted on one row, will be knitted on the next row and stitches that are purled on one row will be purled on the following row. If an odd number of stitches are cast on, every row will begin and end with a knit stitch. The fabric is firm, non-curling and reversible, making it ideal for collars and cuffs.

For an odd number of stitches, the instructions will read:

Pattern row: Knit one stitch, * bring the yarn through the needles to the front of the work, purl the next stitch, take the yarn through the needles to the back of the work, knit the next stitch; repeat from * to end.

Repeat this row to form the pattern.

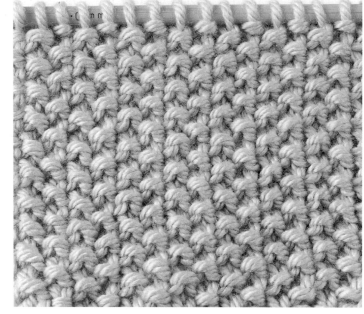

Single rib is formed by alternating knit and purl stitches to form columns of stitches. It produces a very elastic fabric which is ideal for welts, neckbands and borders. It is generally knitted on a smaller needle than the main fabric to keep it firm and elastic.

For an even number of stitches the pattern will be as follows.

1. Knit the first stitch.

2. Bring the yarn through the needles to the front of the work and purl the next stitch (**A**).

3. Take the yarn through the needles to the back of the work and knit the next stitch (**B**).

4. Repeat steps 2 and 3 until all the stitches are on the right-hand needle, ending with a purl stitch.

5. Turn the work and start again from step 1.

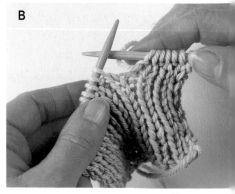

Irish moss stitch is worked over four rows, the first two rows appear the same, then the stitches are alternated on the next two rows. This pattern is often used at the side of Aran stitches.

For an even number of stitches the pattern will be as follows.

1st row: * Knit 1 stitch, purl the next stitch; repeat from * to the end of the row.

2nd row: * Knit 1 stitch, purl the next stitch; repeat from * to the end of the row.

3rd row: * Purl 1 stitch, knit the next stitch; repeat from * to the end of the row.

4th row: * Purl 1 stitch, knit the next stitch; repeat from * to the end of the row.

Repeat rows 1 to 4 to form the pattern.

Double moss stitch is worked over a repeat of four stitches and four rows. It is usually worked over a multiple of four stitches with two extra stitches to balance the pattern.

1st row: Knit the first 2 stitches, * purl the next 2 stitches, knit the next 2 stitches; repeat from * to the end of the row.

2nd row: Purl the first 2 stitches, * knit the next 2 stitches, purl the next 2 stitches; repeat from * to the end of the row.

3rd row: Purl the first 2 stitches, * knit the next 2 stitches, purl the next 2 stitches; repeat from * to the end of the row.

4th row: Knit the first 2 stitches, * purl the next 2 stitches, knit the next 2 stitches; repeat from * to the end of the row.

Repeat rows 1 to 4 to form the pattern.

Double rib is worked over a repeat of four stitches and two rows. It is usually worked over a multiple of four stitches with two extra stitches to balance the pattern.

1st row: Knit the first 2 stitches, * purl the next 2 stitches, knit the next 2 stitches; repeat from * to the end of the row.

2nd row: Purl the first 2 stitches, * knit the next 2 stitches, purl the next 2 stitches; repeat from * to the end of the row.

Repeat rows 1 and 2 to form the pattern.

learn to knit

Cushions and Baby Blanket

Knit the two cushions to practise knitting knit and purl stitches in the same row. Once you are confident that you have mastered the techniques, try something slightly larger and attempt the baby blanket.

BASKET STITCH CUSHION

MEASUREMENTS

32 x 32 cm (12½ x 12½ in)

TENSION

19 stitches and 25 rows to 10 cm (4 in) square measured over stocking stitch using 4½ mm (US 7) needles.

MATERIALS

4 x 50 g balls of Jaeger Merino Aran in grey
Pair of 4½ mm (US 7) knitting needles
Cushion pad, 35 x 35 cm (14 x 14 in)

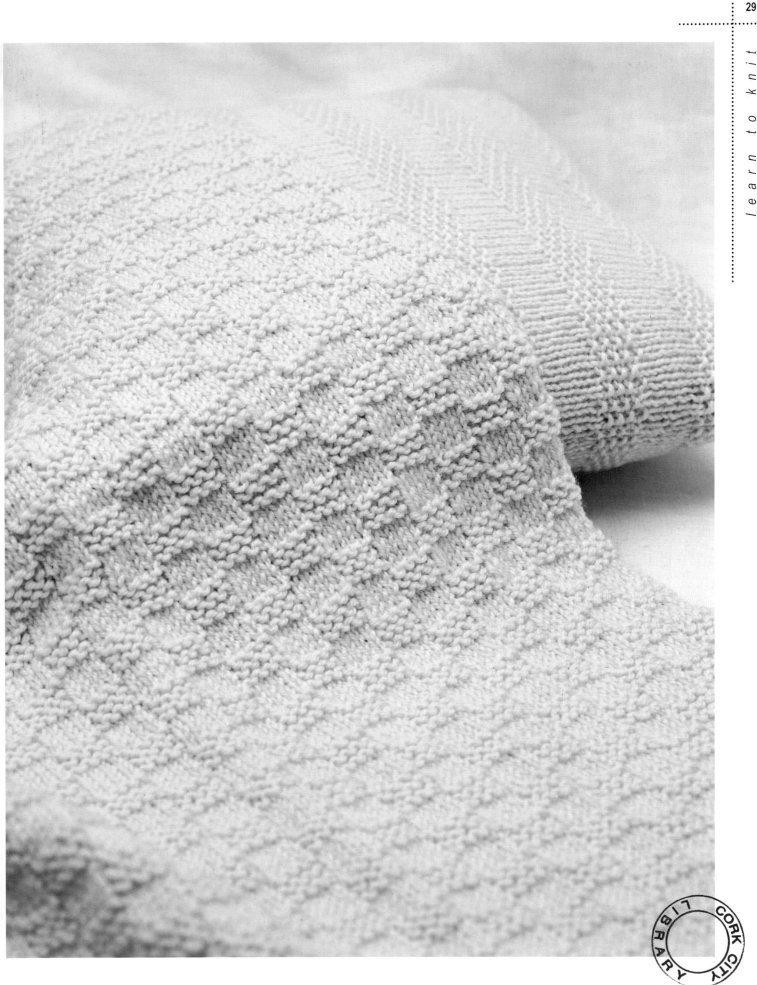

once, then 6th row again.

These 10 rows form the pattern.

Continue in pattern until work measures 32 cm (12½ in) from cast-on edge, ending with 10th row.

Cast off.

Front

Work exactly the same as for the Back.

To Make Up

Sew the two cast-on edges together, then join the two pairs of side edges. Insert cushion pad and join remaining seam to finish.

STOCKING STITCH AND MOSS STITCH CUSHION

MEASUREMENTS

32 x 32 cm (12½ x 12½ in)

MATERIALS

4 x 50 g balls of Jaeger Merino Aran in cream

Pair of 4½ mm (US 7) knitting needles

Cushion pad, 35 x 35 cm (14 x14 in)

TENSION

19 stitches and 25 rows to 10 cm (4 in) square measured over stocking stitch using 4½ mm (US 7) needles.

Back

Cast on 61 stitches.

Begin with a knit row, work 8 rows stocking stitch.

Moss stitch row: Knit 1, ★ purl 1, knit 1; repeat from ★ to end. This row forms the moss stitch pattern.

Work a further 7 rows in moss stitch.

These 16 rows form the pattern.

Continue working in pattern until work measures 32 cm (12½ in) from cast-on edge, ending with 8 rows stocking stitch.

Cast off.

Back

Cast on 60 stitches.

1st row: Knit 4, ★ purl 4, knit 4; repeat from ★ to end.

2nd row: Purl to end.

3rd to 5th rows: Repeat 1st and 2nd rows once, then 1st row again.

6th row: Knit 4, ★ purl 4, knit 4; repeat from ★ to end.

7th row: Knit to end.

8th to 10th rows: Repeat 6th and 7th rows

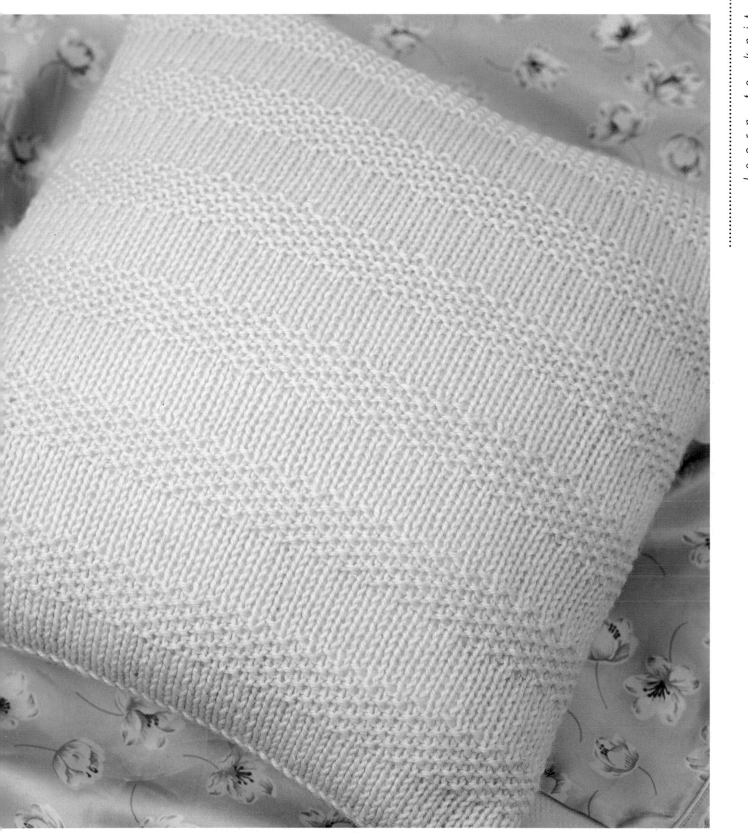

Front

Work exactly the same as for the Back.

To Make Up

Sew the two cast-on edges together, then join the two pairs of side edges. Insert cushion pad and join remaining seam to finish.

BABY BLANKET

MEASUREMENTS

Approximately 47 x 60 cm (18½ in x 23½ in)

TENSION

19 stitches and 32 rows to 10 cm (4 in) measured over pattern using 5 mm (US 8) needles.

MATERIALS

5 x 50 g balls of Jaeger Merino Aran in cream
Pair of 5 mm (US 8) knitting needles

Cast on 92 stitches.

1st row: Knit 4, * purl 4, knit 4; repeat from * to end.

2nd row: Purl to end.

3rd to 5th rows: Repeat 1st and 2nd rows once, then 1st row again.

6th row: Knit 4, * purl 4, knit 4; repeat from * to end.

7th row: Knit to end.

8th to 10th rows: Repeat 6th and 7th rows once, then 6th row again.

These 10 rows form the pattern.

Continue in pattern until blanket measures approximately 60 cm (23½ in) from cast-on edge, ending with 10th row.

Cast off.

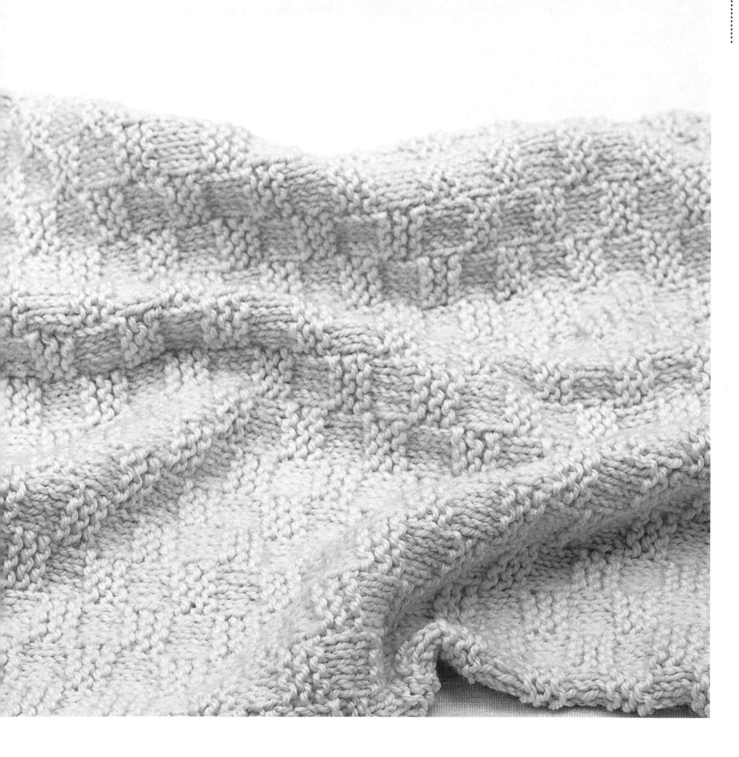

Simple Shaping

The easiest way to shape a garment is by working square corners as this doesn't involve any decreasing or increasing. If the garment is knitted in garter stitch, you do not have to do any extra edgings.

SHAPING A SQUARE NECK

1. Check the pattern to find out how many centimetres or inches to work before you reach the neckline. The instructions will then tell you how to divide the stitches for each part of the neck. Work the number of stitches stated in the pattern, leaving the remaining stitches on a holder or a length of yarn, ready to be worked later.

1

2. The instructions will now tell you what to do with the stitches on the needle to work the first side of the neck. Work straight until the knitting is the required length. Cast off.

2

3. Following the instructions, cast off the centre stitches, then continue to work on the remaining stitches.

3

JOINING SHOULDERS

1. Lay the knitted pieces on a flat surface. Leaving a long end, secure a length of yarn to the first stitch, and insert the needle between the first and second stitches from the back of the work.

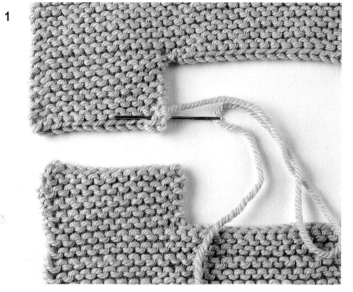

2. Take the needle across to the opposite piece and, from the back, insert between the first and second stitches.

3. Working backwards and forwards from one piece of knitting to the other, insert the needle from the front of the work into the space between the first and second stitch and bring it out in the space between the second and third stitch on the opposite piece.

4. Continue in this way for 5 cm (2 in), then pull the yarn up tight to join the seam close together. Continue in this way to the end of the seam.

5. Secure the ends by oversewing along the seam on the wrong side.

Garter Stitch Jumper

Knit this small jumper using the most simple of shaping methods.

MEASUREMENTS

To fit age	6–12	12–18	18–24	24–36 months
Actual measurements				
Chest	51	56	62	67 cm
	20	22	24½	26½ in
Length to shoulder	28	31	34	38 cm
	11	12¼	13½	15 in
Sleeve length	16	18	21	24 cm
	6¼	7	8¼	9½ in

MATERIALS
5 (5:6:7) x 50 g balls of Debbie Bliss
Merino double knitting in pale pink
Pair of 4 mm (US 6) knitting needles

Before making up a garment, it may be useful to lay out the pieces on a flat surface so you can see how they fit together.

Back

Sleeve

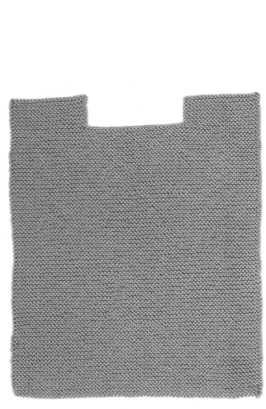

Sleeve

Front

TENSION

22 stitches and 46 rows to 10 cm (4 in) square measured over garter stitch using 4 mm (US 6) needles.

Back

With 4 mm (US 6) needles, cast on 56 (62:68:74) stitches.
Continue in garter stitch until back measures 26 (29:32:36) cm (10¼ (11½:12½:14¼) in) from cast-on edge, ending with a wrong side row.

Shape shoulders and back neck

Knit 16 (18:21:23) stitches, turn and work on this set of stitches only.
Continue straight until back measures 28 (31:34:38) cm (11 (12¼:13½:15) in) from cast-on edge, ending with a wrong side row. Cast off.
With right side facing, rejoin yarn to next stitch, cast off centre 24 (26:26:28) stitches, knit to end.
Continue straight on this group of 16 (18:21:23) stitches until back measures 28 (31:34:38) cm (11 (12¼:13½:15) in) from cast-on edge, ending with a wrong side row. Cast off.

Front

Work as given for Back until front measures 24 (27:30:34) cm (9½ (10½:11¼:13½) in) from cast-on edge, ending with a wrong side row.

Shape shoulders and front neck

Knit 16 (18:21:23) stitches, turn and work on this set of stitches only.
Continue straight until back measures 28 (31:34:38) cm (11 (12½:13½:15) in) from cast-on edge, ending with a wrong side row. Cast off.

NOTE
When working from instructions where there is more than one size, you may find it helpful to go through the instructions and highlight the figures for the size you are making.

With right side facing, rejoin yarn to next stitch, cast off centre 24 (26:26:28) stitches, knit to end.
Continue straight on this group of 16 (18:21:23) stitches until back measures 28 (31:34:38) cm (11 (12¼:13½:15) in) from cast-on edge, ending with a wrong side row. Cast off.

Sleeves

With 4 mm (US 6) needles, cast on 54 (56:58:60) stitches.
Continue in garter stitch until sleeve measures 16 (18:21:24) cm (6¼ (7:8¼:9½) in). Cast off.

To Make Up

Join shoulder seams. Matching centre of sleeve to shoulder seam, sew on sleeves using a back stitch. Join side and sleeve seams, leaving 3 (3:4:4) cm (1¼ (1¼:1½:1½) in) open at lower edge of side seams. Sleeves can be turned up to form a cuff.

Increasing

Increasing, by any one of a number of methods, is used to shape the fabric, making it wider.

KNITTING INTO THE SAME STITCH TWICE

1. On a knit row, knit first into the front of the stitch.

PURLING INTO THE SAME STITCH TWICE

1. On a purl row, purl first into the front of the stitch.

INVISIBLE INCREASING

1. Before working the next stitch on the needle, knit into the stitch below the one on the needle.

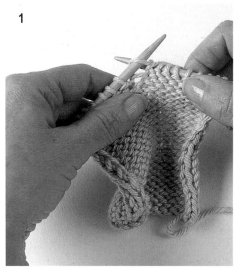

2. Then knit into the back of the same stitch, thus making two stitches from one.

2. Then purl into the back of the same stitch.

2. Then knit into the next stitch on the needle. This method can also be used on a purl row.

RAISED INCREASING

1. Using the right-hand needle, pick up the bar that lies between the stitch just worked on the right-hand needle and the next stitch on the left-hand needle.

1

2. Place the bar on the left-hand needle, twisting it as you do, and knit into the back of it.

2

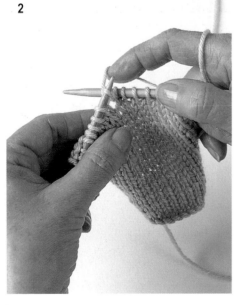

MAKING A STITCH BETWEEN TWO KNIT STITCHES

Bring the the yarn to the front between the needles, then take it over the right-hand needle before knitting the next stitch.

MAKING A STITCH BETWEEN TWO PURL STITCHES

Take the yarn over the right-hand needle to the back of the work, then bring the yarn to the front between the needles.

MAKING A STITCH BETWEEN A KNIT AND A PURL STITCH

Having worked a knit stitch, bring the yarn forward under the right-hand needle, then wind it over the needle and back to the front. Purl the next stitch.

EXTENDING A ROW

Cast on the required number of stitches at the beginning or end of the row, using the usual method.

Child's Jumper with Moss Stitch Borders

Knit this pretty jumper with its moss stitch borders and shaped sleeves.

MEASUREMENTS

To fit age	4-5	6-7	8-9	9-10 years
Actual measurements				
Chest	68	74	80	84 cm
	26¾	29¼	31½	33 in
Length to shoulder	42	44	47	49 cm
	16½	17½	18½	19½ in
Sleeve length	24	26	28	30 cm
	9½	10¼	11	11¾ in

MATERIALS

6 (7:8:9) x 50 g balls of Debbie Bliss wool/cotton in light sage green
Pair each 2¾ mm (US 2) and 3¼ mm (US 3) knitting needles

TENSION

25 stitches and 34 rows to 10 cm (4 in) square measured over stocking stitch using 3¼ mm (US 3) needles.

Back

With 2¾ mm (US 2) needles, cast on 87 (95:103:109) stitches.

1st row: Knit 1, * purl 1, knit 1; rep from * to end.

This row forms the moss stitch pattern.

Repeat this row 7 times more.

Change to 3¼ mm (US 3) needles.

Beginning with a knit row, continue in stocking stitch until Back measures 40 (42:45:47) cm (15¾ (16½:17¾:18½) in) from cast-on edge, ending with a purl row.

Change to 2¾ mm (US 2) needles.

Next row: Knit 1, * purl 1, knit 1; rep from * to end.

This row forms the moss stitch pattern.

Repeat this row 7 times more.

Cast off.

Front

Work exactly the same as for the Back.

Sleeves

With 2¾ mm (US 2) needles cast on 51 (53:57:59) stitches.

Work 8 rows in moss stitch as given for Back.

Change to 3¼ mm (US 3) needles.

Beginning with a knit row, continue in stocking stitch as follows:

Work 4 rows.

Next row: Knit 2, make 1 stitch using the raised increase method, knit to last 2 stitches, make 1 stitch using the raised increase method, knit 2.

Beginning with a purl row, work 3 rows stocking stitch.

Repeat the last 4 rows 16 (17:19:20) times more. 85 (89:97:101) stitches.

Work straight in stocking stitch until sleeve measures 24 (26:28:30) cm (9½ (10¼:11:11¾) in) from cast-on edge, ending with a purl row.

Cast off.

To Make Up

Join shoulder seams for 10 (11:12:13) cm (4 (4¼:4¾:5) in). Sew on sleeves using a backstitch. Using the invisible seam method (see below), join side and sleeve seams, leaving the moss stitch borders at the lower edge of the side seams open.

Invisible seaming

This is the method most knitters use to obtain a professional finish. The seam is particularly suitable for straight stocking stitch edges. You work from the front, so you can see exactly what you are doing.

1. With the right sides of both pieces of fabric facing upwards, join in the yarn, and thread the needle under the horizontal strand linking the edge stitch and the next stitch. Pass the needle under one row, then bring it to the front.

2. Return to the opposite side and, working under one row at a time throughout, repeat this zig-zag action. Always take the needle under one row and insert it back into the hole that the last stitch on that side came out of. After you have worked 5 cm (2 in), pull the yarn up tight, so the work is pulled together creating a seam.

Decreasing

Decreasing, by any one of a number of methods,
is used to reduce the number of stitches, making
the fabric narrower

BASIC DECREASING

This is the simplest and most commonly
used method.

1. Insert the right-hand needle from left to
right through the second then the first stitch
on the left-hand needle.

1

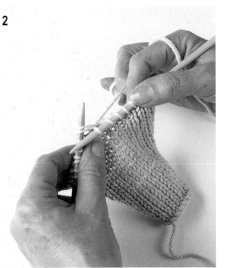

2. Knit the two stitches together, making one.

2

PURL DECREASING

1. Insert the right-hand needle from right to
left through the first two stitches on the left-
hand needle.

1

2. Purl the two stitches together, making one
stitch.

2

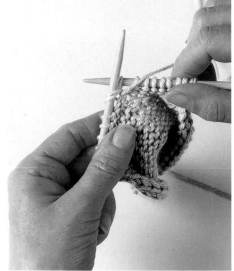

SLIP STITCH DECREASING

1. Slip a stitch from the left-hand needle on
to the right-hand needle. Knit the next stitch.

1

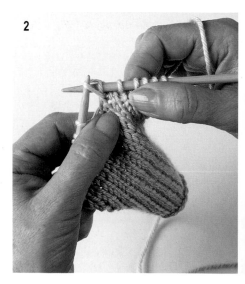

2. Then, using the tip of the left-hand needle,
pass the slipped stitch over the last stitch
on the right-hand needle and drop it off the
needle.

2

Basic Buttonholes

A buttonhole is a small closed slit worked in a border, used for fastening a button. It needs to be worked neatly or it will stretch and become non-functional. When following a pattern you will be told how many buttonholes to make and how far apart.

EYELET BUTTONHOLES

These are the simplest buttonholes to make and are suitable for fine yarns and baby clothes.

Worked in garter stitch

1. Knit to the position of the buttonhole, then knit the next two stitches together.

1

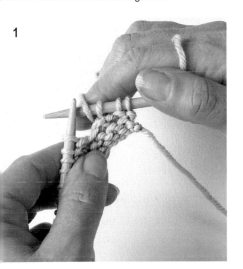

2. Bring the yarn between the needles to the front of the work.

2

Worked in rib

1. Work in rib to the position of the button-hole, bring the yarn between the needles and take back over the right-hand needle.

1

2. Either knit or purl the next two stitches together to keep the rib pattern correct.

2

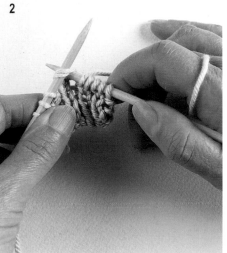

Worked in moss stitch

1. Work in moss stitch to the position of the buttonhole, bring the yarn between the needles and take back over the right-hand needle. Work the next two stitches together to keep the pattern correct.

1

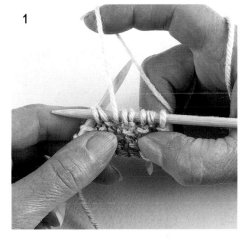

2. A small neat buttonhole is formed.

2

Cardigan with Garter Stitch and Stocking Stitch Stripes

With its simple shaping and buttonholes, this is ideal for your first "adult" project.

MEASUREMENTS

To fit	81	86	91 cm
	32	34	36 in

Actual measurements

Bust	91	96	101 cm
	35¾	37¾	39¾ in
Length to shoulder	55	55	55 cm
	21½	21½	21½ in
Sleeve length	46	46	46 cm
	18	18	18 in

MATERIALS

10 (11:12) x 50 g balls of Jaeger Merino Double Knitting in cream
Pair each 3¼ mm (US 3) and 4 mm (US 6) knitting needles
6 buttons

TENSION

22 stitches and 30 rows to 10 cm (4 in) square measured over stocking stitch using 4 mm (US 6) needles.

Back

With 3¼ mm (US 3) needles, cast on 102 (107:112) stitches.
Knit 9 rows.
Change to 4 mm (US 6) needles.
Beginning with a knit row, work 8 rows in stocking stitch.
Knit 10 rows.
Repeat the last 18 rows 9 times more.
Cast off.

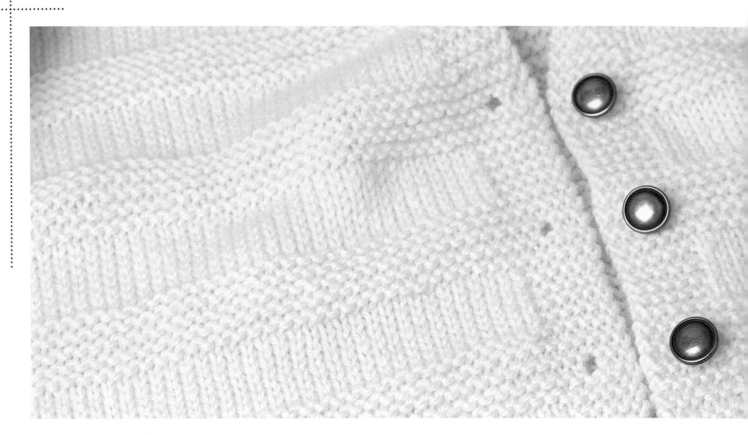

Left Front

With 3¼ mm (US 3) needles, cast on 54 (57:60) stitches.

Knit 9 rows.

Change to 4 mm (US 6) needles.

Work in pattern with 6 stitches in garter stitch at centre front edge as follows:

1st row: Knit to end.

2nd row: Knit 6, purl to end.

Repeat the last 2 rows 3 times more.

Knit 10 rows.

Repeat the last 18 rows four times more.

Now work in pattern, shaping front edge for neck as follows:

1st row: Knit to last 7 stitches, knit 2 stitches together, knit 5.

2nd row: Knit 6, purl to end.

3rd row: Knit to end.

4th row: Knit 6, purl to end.

5th to 8th rows: Repeat 1st to 4th rows once more.

9th row: Knit to last 7 stitches, knit 2 stitches together, knit 5.

10th row: Knit to end.

11th row: Knit to end.

12th row: Knit to end.

13th row to 16th row: Repeat 9th to 12th rows once more.

17th row: Knit to end.

18th row: Knit to end.

Repeat the last 18 rows 3 times more. 38 (41:44) stitches.

Now work the 1st to 8th rows of neck shaping. 36 (39:42) stitches.

Knit 10 rows.

Now cast off for shoulder as follows:

Cast off first 30 (33:36) stitches, then knit remaining 6 stitches.

Continue in garter stitch on these stitches for a further 9 cm (3½ in) for back neck border. Cast off.

Right Front

With 3¼ mm (US 3) needles, cast on 54 (57:60) stitches.

Knit 3 rows.

Buttonhole row: Knit 2, knit 2 stitches together, bring the yarn to the front between the needles, then take over the right-hand needle, knit to end.

Knit 5 rows.

Change to 4 mm (US 6) needles.

Work in pattern with 6 stitches in garter stitch at centre front edge as follows:

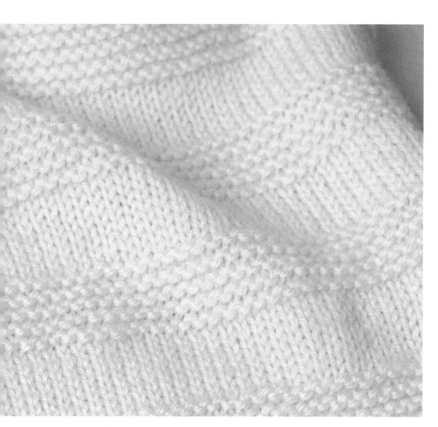

1st row: Knit to end.

2nd row: Purl to last 6 stitches, knit 6.

Repeat the last 2 rows 3 times more.

Knit 4 rows.

Buttonhole row: Knit 2, knit 2 stitches together, bring the yarn to the front between the needles, then take over the right-hand needle, knit to end.

Knit 5 rows.

Repeat the last 18 rows 4 times more.

Now work in pattern, shaping front edge for neck as follows:

1st row: Knit 5, slip next stitch, knit next stitch, then pass the slipped stitch over the knitted stitch and off the needle, knit to end.

2nd row: Purl to last 6 sts, knit 6.

3rd row: Knit to end.

4th row: Purl to last 6 sts, knit 6.

5th to 8th rows: Repeat 1st to 4th rows once more.

9th row: Knit 5, slip next stitch, knit next stitch, then pass the slipped stitch over the knitted stitch and off the needle, knit to end.

10th row: Knit to end.

11th row: Knit to end.

12th row: Knit to end.

13th row to 16th row: Repeat 9th to 12th rows once more.

17th row: Knit to end.

18th row: Knit to end.

Repeat the last 18 rows 3 times more. 38 (41:44) stitches.

Now work the 1st to 8th rows of neck shaping. 36 (39:42) stitches.

Knit 10 rows.

Now cast off for shoulder as follows:

Knit 6 stitches, cast off remaining 30 (33:36) stitches.

With wrong side facing, join yarn to remaining 6 stitches.

Continue in garter stitch on these stitches for a further 9 cm (3¼ in) for back neck border. Cast off.

Sleeves

With 3¼ mm (US 3) needles, cast on 46 (50:54) stitches.

Knit 9 rows.

Change to 4 mm (US 6) needles.

1st row: Knit 3, make 1 stitch using raised increasing method, knit to last 3 stitches, make 1 stitch using raised increasing method, knit 3.

2nd row: Purl to end.

3rd row: Knit to end.

4th row: Purl to end.

5th to 8th rows: Repeat 1st to 4th rows once more.

9th row: Knit 3, make 1 stitch using raised increasing method, knit to last 3 stitches, make 1 stitch using raised increasing method, knit 3.

10th to 13th rows: Knit to end.

14th to 18th rows: Repeat 9th to 13th rows once more.

Repeat the last 18 rows 6 times more. 102 (106:110) stitches.

Pattern a further 18 rows.

Cast off.

To Make Up

Join shoulder seams. Join cast off edges of neck border. Sew neck border to back neck. With centre of sleeve to shoulder seam, sew on sleeves, using a back stitch. Using the invisible seam method, join side and sleeve seams (see page 44). Sew on buttons.

Stocking Stitch Sweater with Raglan Shaping

So far all the instructions have been written out in full. The following instructions are given in full with the common abbreviation in bold.

MEASUREMENTS

To fit age	2-3	3-4	4-5 years

Actual measurements

Chest	71	80	90 cm
	28	31½	35½ in
Length	35	40	45 cm
	13¾	15¾	17¾ in
Sleeve length	22	25	28 cm
	8¾	10	11 in

MATERIALS

7 (7:8) x 50 g balls of Debbie Bliss Merino Aran in bright red
Pair each 3¾ mm (US 5) and 4½ mm (US 7) needles

TENSION

18 sts and 26 rows to 10 cm (4 in) square measured over stocking stitch **st st** using 4½ mm (US 7) needles.

Back and Front (both alike)

With 3¾ mm (US 5) needles, cast on 66 (74:82) stitches **sts**.
Knit **K** 9 rows.
Change to 4½ mm (US 7) needles.
Begin **Beg** with a knit **k** row, work in stocking stitch **st st** until back measures 20 (22:24) cm (8 (8¾:9½) in) from cast-on edge, ending with a purl **p** row.

Shape raglan armhole

Cast off 5 (6:7) stitches **sts** at begining **beg** of next 2 rows. 56 (62:68) stitches **sts**.
1st row: Knit **K** 3 stitches **sts**, slip **sl** 1 stitch, knit **k** 1 stitch, pass slipped stitch over **skpo**, knit **k** to last 5 stitches **sts**, knit 2 stitches together **k2 tog**, knit **k** 3.

2nd row: Purl **P** to end.
Rep the last 2 rows until 20 (22:24) **sts** rem, ending with a purl **p** row.
Change to 3¾ mm (US 5) needles.
Knit **K** 8 rows.
Cast off.

Sleeves

With 3¾ mm (US 5) needles, cast on 38 (42:46) stitches **sts**.
Knit **K** 9 rows.
Change to 4½ mm (US 7) needles.
Beginning **Beg** with a knit **k** row, continue **cont** in stocking stitch **st st**.
Work 4 rows.
Inc row: Knit **K** 3 stitches **sts**, pick up the bar between the stitch **st** just worked and the next stitch **st** on left hand needle and work into the back of it **m1**, knit **k** to last 3 stitches **sts**, pick up the bar between the stitch **st** just worked and the next stitch **st** on left hand needle and work into the back of it **m1**, knit **k** 3 stitches **sts**.
Beginning **Beg** with a purl **p** row, work 3 rows stocking stitch **st st**.
Repeat **Rep** the last 4 rows until there are 60 (66:72) stitches **sts**.
Continue **Cont** straight until sleeve measures 22 (25:28) cm (8¾ (10:11) in) from cast-on edge, ending with a wrong side **WS** row.

Raglan shapings may look difficult, but laid out flat it is easy to see how they go together. With "fully fashioned" shapings the seams can be joined using the invisible seaming method.

back

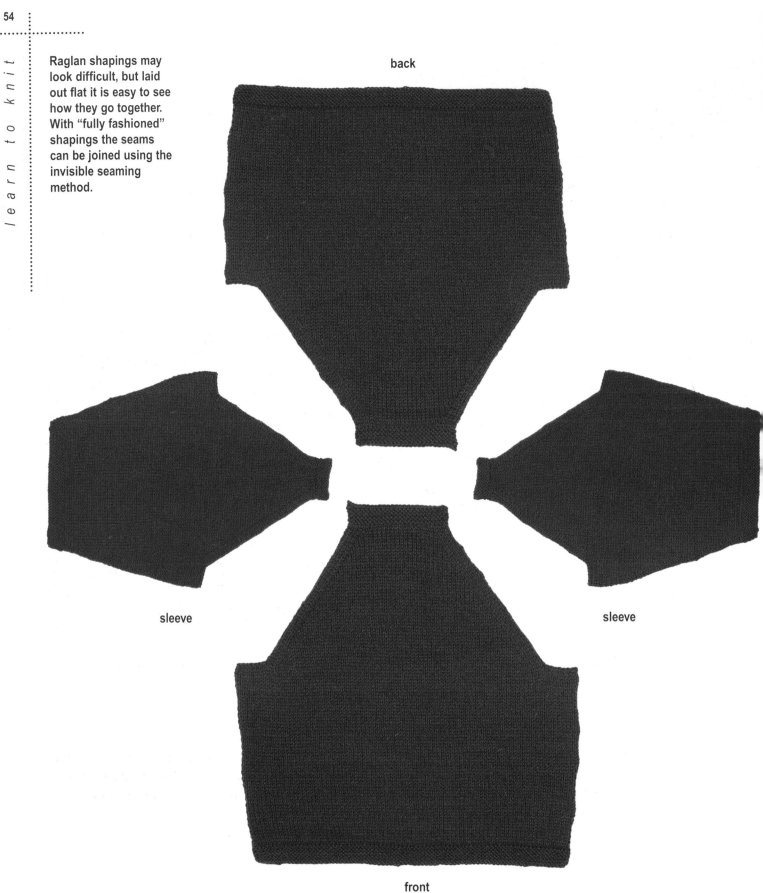

sleeve

sleeve

front

Shape raglan top

Cast off 5 (6:7) stitches **sts** at beg of next 2 rows. 50 (54:58) stitches **sts**.

1st row: Knit **K** 3 stitches **sts**, slip 1 stitch, knit 1 stitch, pass slipped stitch over **skpo**, knit **k** to last 5 stitches **sts**, knit 2 stitches together **k2 tog**, knit **k** 3.

2nd row: Purl **P** to end.

Repeat **Rep** the last 2 rows until 14 stitches **sts** remain **rem**, ending with a purl **p** row.

Change to 3¾ mm (US 5) needles.
Knit **K** 8 rows.
Cast off.

To Make Up

Using the invisible seam method (see page 44), join raglan and neckband seams. Join side and sleeve seams using the same method.

Working from a Chart

Working from a chart is usually associated with colour knitting, but simple textured motifs can also be worked from a chart.

MOTIF PATTERNS

These can either be written out in full, row by row, or drawn out in a chart form. The advantages of having a chart are that the motif is instantly visible and that space is saved in the pattern instructions.

These can be worked in stocking stitch on a reversed stocking stitch background, reversed stocking stitch on a stocking stitch background, or moss stitch on either stocking stitch or reversed stocking stitch backgrounds.

The charts on these pages have a very simple key. A blank square indicates that a knit stitch should be used on a right side row and a purl stitch on a wrong side row. The second symbol indicates that a purl stitch should be used on a right side row and a knit stitch on a wrong side row.

ROWS

When reading the chart, odd numbered rows which are numbered up the right-hand side of the chart at are right side rows, are read from right to left, even numbered rows, which may be numbered up the left-hand side of the chart are wrong side rows, are read from left to right.

STITCHES

Usually only one repeat of the pattern is given in the chart, the stitches which form the repeat are usually indicated by the words "repeat these stitches". Any stitches that will not divide into the pattern are charted either side of the pattern repeat and are knitted at the beginning and ends of the rows to balance the pattern.

Start reading the chart from the bottom right-hand corner, the first square is the first stitch of the first row.

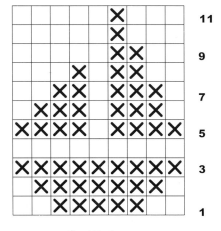

9 stitches

SOME MORE MOTIFS. These motifs can be used on their own, placing them at the centre of the chest or in the corner of a garment, something like the boat could be placed on the sleeve. The motifs could also be "joined" together to form a border.

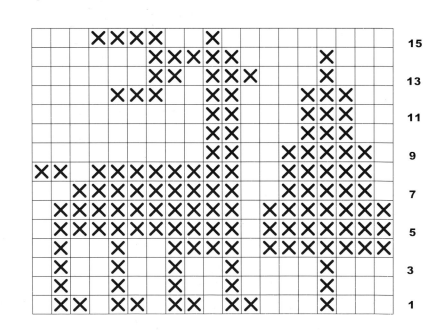

19 stitches

KEY

☐	k on right side and p on wrong side
☒	p on right side and k on wrong side

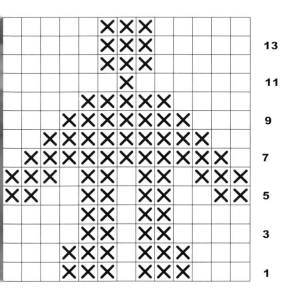

13 stitches

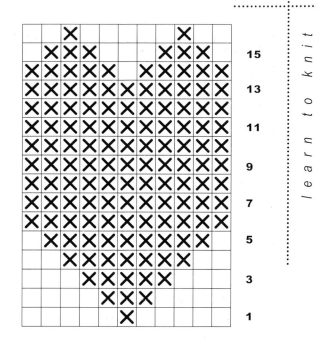

11 stitches

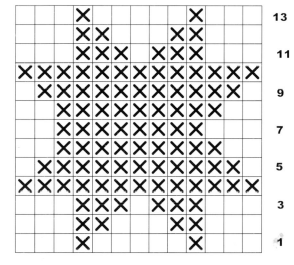

13 stitches

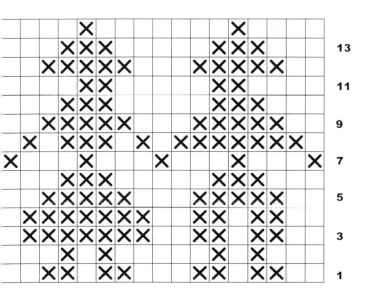

17 stitches

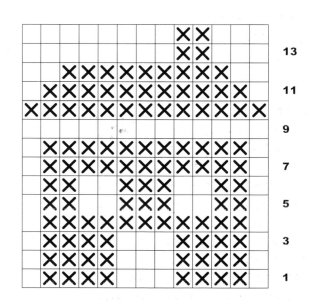

13 stitches

Picking up Stitches

**Most edges of a knitted fabric will curl unless a border is
knitted on after the garment is completed.**

Once the main body of the knitting is compete, it is often necessary to pick up stitches to work a border; this might be a neckband, collar, front edging, cuffs or armbands. The technique of picking up stitches along an edge is referred to as "pick up and knit", as stitches are made with new yarn rather than the loops of the main fabric.

When working from a pattern you will be told how many stitches to pick up. Great care must be taken to ensure that the stitches are picked up evenly along the edge, otherwise the fabric will buckle. A simple way to do this is to divide the edge into sections using pins. For instance, divide the edge evenly into eight sections. Then divide the number of stitches to be picked up by eight and pick up this number of stitches in each section, checking the total number of stitches at the end.

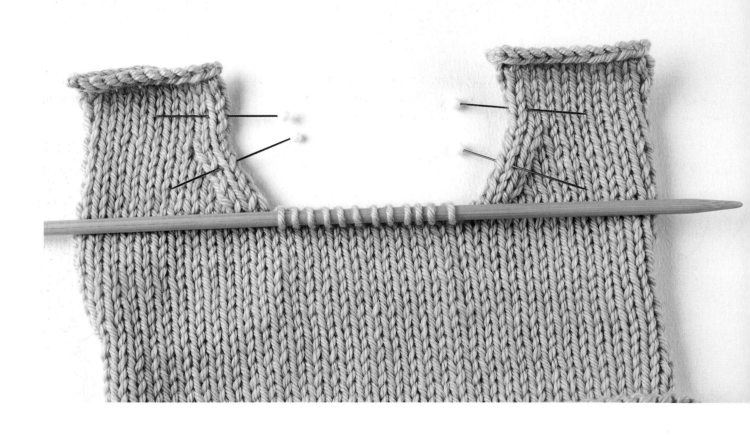

WORKING ALONG A CAST-ON OR CAST-OFF EDGE

1. With right side facing and holding a needle in your right hand, insert the point from front to back under both loops of the cast-on or cast-off edge. Wind the yarn round the needle as though knitting a stitch.

WORKING ALONG A SIDE EDGE

1. With right side facing and holding a needle in your right hand, insert the point from front to back between the first and second stitch in from the edge. Wind the yarn round the needle as though knitting a stitch.

WORKING BORDERS

These are usually worked on a smaller needle than the main body of the garment.

1. A garter stitch border is often worked along a front edge of a garment; this is especially suitable if a zip is going to be inserted.

2. Draw a loop through, forming a stitch on the needle. Continue in this way until the required number of stitches are picked up.

2. Draw a loop through, forming a stitch on the needle. Continue in this way until the required number of stitches are picked up.

2. Rib borders are most often used as an edging where a garment requires buttonholes to be added.

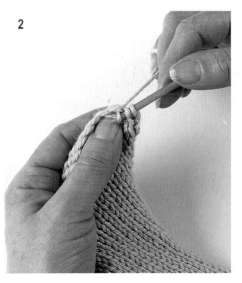

Motif Jumper

This simple cream jumper has a row of star motifs joined together to make a border.

MEASUREMENTS

To fit age	1-2	2-3	3-4 years

Actual measurements

Chest	70	77	84 cm
	27½	30¼	33 in

Length to shoulder

	36	40	44 cm
	14¼	15¾	17¾ in

Sleeve length

	22	24	27 cm
	8¾	9½	10½ in

MATERIALS

6 (6:7) x 50 g balls Rowan Wool/Cotton in cream
Pair each 3¾ mm (US 5) and 4 mm (US 6) knitting needles

TENSION

22 sts and 30 rows to 10 cm (4 in) square measured over st st using 4 mm (US 6) needles.

ABBREVIATIONS

beg	beginning
cm	centimetres
cont	continue
dec	decrease(ing)
folls	follows
in	inches
inc	increase(ing)
k	knit
mm	millimetres
p	purl
patt	pattern
rem	remain(ing)
rep	repeat
st(s)	stitch(es)
st st	stocking stitch, k on right side and p on wrong side

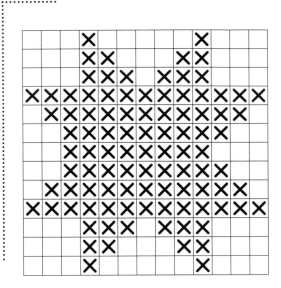

KEY

 k on right side and p on wrong side

 p on right side and k on wrong side

Back

With 3¾ mm (US 5) needles, cast on 78 (86:94) sts.

1st row: K2, * p2, k2; rep from * to end.

2nd row: P2, * k2, p2; rep from * to end.

Rep the last 2 rows 2 (2:3) times more.

Change to 4 mm (US 6) needles.

Dec row: K to end, dec one st at centre. 77 (85:93) sts.

Next row: P to end.

Next row: K to end.

Next row: P to end.

Next row: P to end.

Next row: K to end.

Next row: K to end.

Next row: P to end.

Now work in patt as folls:

Next row: K4 (1:5) sts, now reading chart from right to left work across 1st row 5 (6:6) times, k3 (0:4) sts.

Next row: P3 (0:4) sts, now reading chart from left to right work across 2nd row 5 (6:6) times, p4 (1:5) sts.

Next row: K4 (1:5) sts, now reading chart from right to left work across 3rd row 5 (6:6) times, k3 (0:4) sts.

Next row: P3 (0:4) sts, now reading chart from left to right work across 4th row 5 (6:6) times, p4 (1:5) sts.

Cont in this way until all 13 rows have been worked.

Next row: P to end.

Next row: K to end.

Next row: K to end.

Next row: P to end.

Beg with a p row, cont in st st until back measures 36 (40:44) cm (14¼ (15¾ :17¾) in) from cast-on edge, ending with a p row.

Shape shoulders

Cast off 25 (28:31) sts at beg of next 2 rows.

Leave rem 27 (29:31) sts on a spare needle.

Front

Work as given for Back until front measures 30 (33:36) cm (11¾ (13:14) in) from cast-on edge, ending with a p row.

Shape neck

Next row: K30 (33:36), turn and work on these sts for first side of neck.

Dec one st at neck edge on every row until 25 (28:31) sts rem.

Work straight until front matches back to shoulder shaping, ending at side edge.

Shape shoulder

Cast off.

With right side facing, slip centre 17 (19:21) sts onto a spare needle, rejoin yarn to rem sts, k to end.

Dec one st at neck edge on every row until 25 (28:31) sts rem.

Work straight until front matches back to shoulder shaping, ending at side edge.

Shape shoulder

Cast off.

Sleeves

With 3¾ mm (US 5) needles cast on 50 (54:58) sts.

1st row: K2, * p2, k2; rep from * to end.

2nd row: P2, * k2, p2; rep from * to end.

Rep the last 2 rows 2 (2:3) times more.

Change to 4 mm (US 6) needles.

Beg with a k row, cont in st st, inc 1 st at each end of the 3rd and every foll 4th row until there are 74 (82:90) sts on the needle.

Now work straight until the sleeve measures

22 (24:27) cm (8¾ (9½:10½) in) from cast-on edge, ending with a p row.
Cast off.

Neckband
Join the right shoulder seam.
With 3¾ mm (US 5) needles, and right side facing, pick up and k15 (17:19) sts down left side of front neck, k across 17 (19:21) sts from front neck holder, pick up and k15 (17:19) sts up right side of front neck, k across 27 (29:31) sts from back neck holder. 74 (82:90) sts.

Next row: K2, * p2, k2; rep from * to end.
Next row: P2, * k2, p2; rep from * to end.
Rep the last 2 rows twice more.
Cast off in rib.

To Make Up
Join left shoulder seam and neckband.
With centre of sleeve to shoulder seam, sew on sleeves. Using the invisible seam method (see page 44), join side and sleeve seams.

More Buttonholes

When making a garment in thicker yarn or if you wish to use larger buttons, larger buttonholes are also required. Specific instructions will be given in the pattern.

VERTICAL BUTTONHOLES

These can be used for jackets made with thick yarn where big buttons are required.

1. Work to the position of the buttonhole. Join in another ball of yarn to the stitches on the left-hand needle.

3. When the buttonhole is the required depth, close the gap by working across both sets of stitches with the first ball. Leaving a long end, cut off the second ball. To complete the buttonhole, use the ends from the second ball of yarn to strengthen the corners, then darn in the ends.

2. On the next row, work to the cast-off stitches. Turn the work and cast on the same number of stitches using the cable method, but before placing the last cast-on stitch on to the left-hand needle, bring the yarn to the front between the stitches.

2. Continue to work each side separately with their own balls of yarn.

HORIZONTAL BUTTONHOLES

These are worked over two rows and used on cardigans and waistcoats.

1. On a right side row, work to the position of the start of the buttonhole. Working in pattern, cast off the required number of stitches, then work to the end of the row.

3. Turn the work and complete the row.

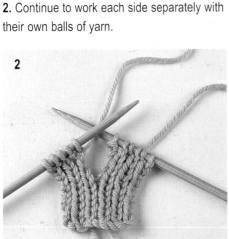

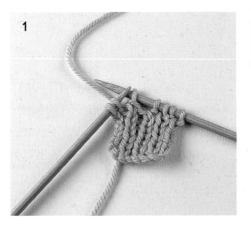

Working in Stripes

The simplest way of introducing a second colour into knitting is to work in stripes. You will need to carry the yarn up the side of the knitting; this will save you from cutting off and joining in new balls of yarn every time you change colour.

CREATING STRIPES

1. Using the second colour work a simple knot around the first colour before starting to knit the row.

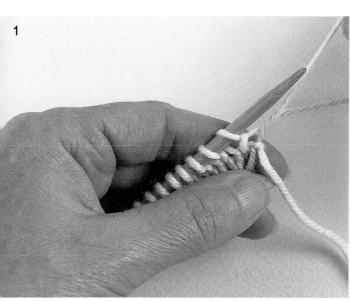

2. Before starting the next knit row, take the second colour around the first colour so "carrying" the first colour up the side.

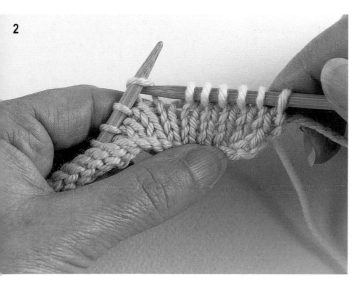

3. When the stripe is the required depth, bring the first colour around the second colour so that it is ready to start knitting with.

4. The "wrong" side of the fabric can also be used, the stripe is not so defined and you get a more subtle colour change over.

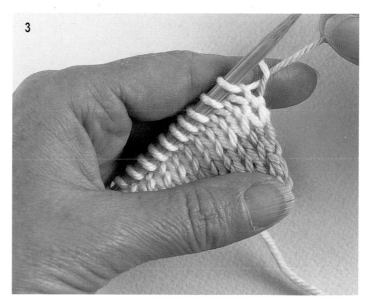

Striped Cushions

These classic striped cushions, worked in stocking stitch, look great in smart greys and creams, especially when piled up on a sofa with lots of other cushions

MEASUREMENTS

33 x 33 cm (13 x 13 in)

MATERIALS

4 x 50 g balls Jaeger Merino Aran (2 of each colour)
Cushion pad 35 x 35 cm (14 x 14 in)
Pair of 4½ mm (US 7) knitting needles

TENSION

19 stitches and 25 rows to 10 cm (4 in) square over stocking stitch using 4½ mm (US 7) needles.

Back

Using first colour, cast on 63 stitches.
1st row Using first colour knit to end.
2nd row Using first colour purl to end.
3rd row Using first colour knit to end.
4th row Using first colour purl to end.
Join in second colour.
5th row Using second colour knit to end.
6th row Using second colour purl to end.
7th row Using second colour knit to end.
8th row Using second colour purl to end.
These eight rows form the stocking stitch pattern and stripe sequence.
Continue in striped stocking stitch until work measures 33 cm (13 in) from cast-on edge, ending with 4 rows in one colour.
Cast off.

Front

Work exactly the same as the Back.

To Make Up

Sew two cast-on edges together, then join two pairs of side edges. Insert cushion pad and join remaining seam.

Striped Jacket

The easiest way of introducing colour is to work in stripes.

MEASUREMENTS

To fit	4-5	6-7	8-9	9-10 years
Actual measurements				
Chest	69	76	83	88 cm
	27	30	33	35 in
Length to shoulder	38	41	44	47 cm
	15	16	17¼	18½ in
Sleeve length	30	33	35	38 cm
	1¾	13	13¾	15 in

MATERIALS

4 (4:5:5) x 50 g balls of Debbie Bliss
Merino Aran in navy and
4 (4:4:5) x 50 g balls in cream
Pair each 4½ mm (US 7) and 5 mm
(US 8) knitting needles
6 buttons

TENSION

18 sts and 24 rows to 10 cm (4 in) measured
over st st using 5 mm (US 8) needles.

ABBREVIATIONS

beg	beginning
cm	centimetres
cont	continue
in	inches
k	knit
m1	make 1 st by picking up the bar between the st just worked and the next st on left-hand needle and working into the back of it
mm	millimetres
p	purl
patt	pattern
rem	remain(ing)
rep	repeat
skpo	slip 1, knit 1, pass slipped st over
st(s)	stitch(es)
st st	stocking stitch, k on right side and p back
tog	together

Back

With 4½ mm (US 7) needles and Navy, cast on
64 (70:76:82) sts.
K 5 rows.
Change to 5 mm (US 8) needles.

Now work in stripe patt as follows:
Join in Cream.
Using Cream and beg with a k row, work
4 rows in st st.
Join in Navy.
Using Navy and beg with a k row work 4 rows
in st st.
Cont in stripes of 4 rows Cream and 4 rows
Navy until Back measures 38 (41:44:47) cm
(15 (16:17¼:18½) in) from cast-on edge, end-
ing with a wrong side row.

Shape shoulders
Cast off 21 (23:25:27) sts at the beg of the
next 2 rows.
Change to 4½ mm (US 7) needles.
Using Navy knit 6 rows.
Cast off.

Left front
With 4½ mm (US 7) needles and Navy cast on
32 (35:38:41) sts.
K 5 rows.
Change to 5 mm (US 8) needles.
Now work in stripe patt as follows:
Join in Cream.
Using Cream and beg with a k row, work
4 rows in st st.
Join in Navy.
Using Navy and beg with a k row, work 4 rows
in st st.
Cont in stripes of 4 rows Cream and 4 rows
Navy until Front measures 25 (27:29:31) cm
(10 (10¾:11½ :12¼) in) from cast-on edge,
ending with a wrong side row.
Mark beginning of last row with a coloured
thread. This denotes the beg of the neck shap-
ing and will be useful when picking up
stitches for the front band.

Shape front neck
Working in stripes, cont as follows:
Next row: K to the last 4 sts, k2 tog, k2.
Next row: P to end.

Repeat the last 2 rows until 21 (23:25:27) sts rem.

Now work straight until the same number of rows have been worked as on the Back to shoulder, ending with a wrong side row.

Cast off.

Right Front

With 4½ mm (US 7) needles and Navy cast on 32 (35:38:41) sts.

K 5 rows.

Change to 5 mm (US 8) needles.

Now work in stripe pattern as follows:

Join in Cream.

Using Cream and beg with a k row, work 4 rows in st st.

Join in Navy.

Using Navy and beg with a k row, work 4 rows in st st.

Cont in stripes of 4 rows Cream and 4 rows Navy until Front measures 25 (27:29:31) cm (10 (10¾:11½ :12¼) in) from cast-on edge, ending with a wrong side row.

Mark end of last row with a coloured thread. This denotes the beg of the neck shaping and will be useful when picking up stitches for the front band.

Shape front neck

Working in stripes, cont as follows:

Next row: K2, skpo, k to end.

Next row: P to end.

Rep the last 2 rows until 21 (23:25:27) sts remain.

Now work straight until the same number of rows have been worked as on the Back to shoulder, ending with a right side row.

Cast off.

Sleeves

With 4½ mm (US 7) needles and Navy, cast on 32 (34:36:38) sts.

K 5 rows.

Change to 5 mm (US 8) needles.

Now work in stripe patt and shape sides as follows:

Join in Cream.

Using Cream and beg with a k row work 2 rows in st st.

Next row: K2, m1, k to last 2 sts, m1, k2.

P 1 row.

Join in Navy.

Using Navy and beg with a k row work 2 rows in st st.

Next row: K2, m1, k to last 2 sts, m1, k2.

P 1 row.

Rep the last 8 rows until there are 62 (68:74:80) sts on the needle.

Cont straight until sleeve measures 30 (33:35:38) cm (11¾ (13:13¾:15) in) from cast-on edge, ending with a wrong side row.

Cast off.

Buttonhole band

Using 4½ mm (US 7) needles and with right side facing and Navy, pick up and k50 (54:58:62) sts along right front edge to beg of neck shaping, then 32 (34:36:38) sts to shoulder. 82 (88:94:100) sts.

K 2 rows.

Buttonhole row: K37 (38:39:40) sts, [k2 tog, yf, k6 (7,8,9) sts] 5 times, k2 tog, yf, k3.

K 2 rows.

Cast off.

Button band

Using 4½ mm (US 7) needles and with right side facing and Navy, pick up and k32 (34:36:38) sts along left front edge from shoulder to beginning of neck shaping, then 50 (54:58:62) sts to cast-on edge. 82 (88:94:100) sts.

K 5 rows.

Cast off.

To Make Up

Join shoulder seams, carrying seam on through neck edgings. With centre of sleeve to shoulder seam, sew on sleeves. Using the invisible seam method (see page 44), join side and sleeve seams. Sew on buttons.

Pockets

Many garments feature pockets for both practical and decorative purposes. These fall into two categories – patch pockets, which are added afterwards, and those which are an integral part of the garment. Precise instructions are given with working patterns.

PATCH POCKETS

These are pockets added to the right side of a garment.

1. Mark where the pocket is to be positioned with contrast threads.

2. Pin the pocket in position on the background, lining the pockets up with rows and stitches. Using a slip stitch, sew the pockets in place.

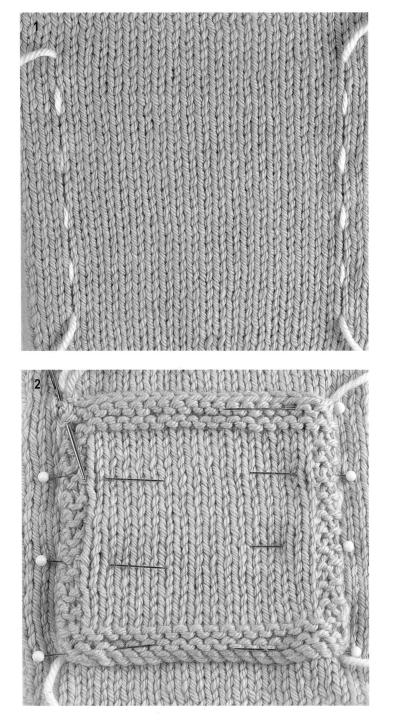

HORIZONTAL POCKETS

A horizontal pocket is knitted into the garment as an integral part of the design.

1. Make the lining in st st, ending with a p row. Cut off the yarn and slip the sts on to a holder. Work in pattern on the main part until you reach the pocket opening, ending on a wrong side row. **Next row:** work to pocket position and leave the group of stitches for the pocket on a length of yarn.

2. Work across the stitches of pocket lining, work to end of row.

3. When the garment is completed, the stitches on the length of yarn are worked in pattern to neaten the top. Sew down row ends.

4. Pin the pocket lining in place on the wrong side and slip stitch in position.

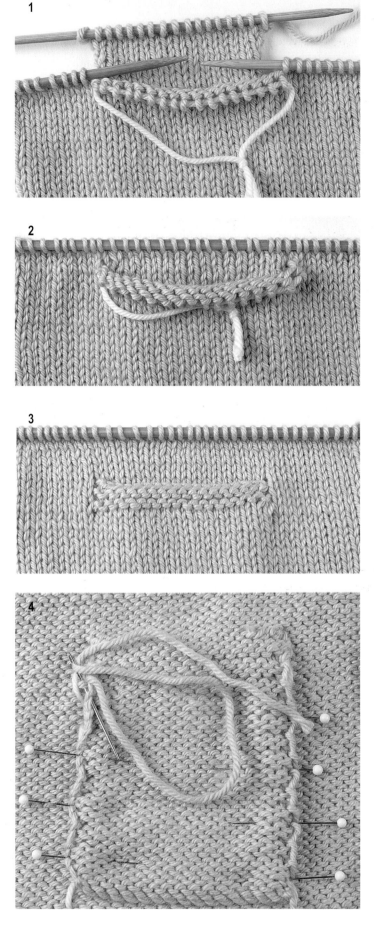

Tunic with Pockets

Pockets are very easy to do when you follow
these clear instructions.

MEASUREMENTS

To fit bust	82	87	92 cm
	32	34	36 in

Actual measurements			
Bust	104	108	112 cm
	41	42½	44 in
Length to shoulder	52	54	56 cm
	20½	21¼	22 in
Sleeve length	46	46	48 cm
	18	18	19 in

MATERIALS

13 (14:15) x 50 g balls of Debbie Bliss Merino
Aran in dark grey or claret
Pair each 4½ mm (US 7) and 5 mm (US 8)
knitting needles

TENSION

18 sts and 24 rows to 10 cm (4 in) square over
st st using 5 mm (US 8) needles.

ABBREVIATIONS

beg	beginning
cm	centimetres
cont	continue
dec	decrease(ing)
in	inches
inc	increase(ing)
k	knit
m1	make 1 st by picking up the bar between the st just worked and the next st on left-hand needle and working into the back of it
mm	millimetres
p	purl
rem	remain(ing)
rep	repeat
st(s)	stitch(es)
st st	stocking stitch, k on right side and p back

Back

With 4½ mm (US 7) needles cast on 96 (100:104) sts.

K 7 rows.

Change to 5 mm (US 8) needles.

Beg with a k row, cont in st st until back measures 52 (54:56) cm (20½ (21¼:22) in) from cast-on edge, ending with a p row.

Shape shoulders

Cast off 33 (35:37) sts at beg of next 2 rows.

Leave rem 30 sts on a spare needle.

Pocket Linings (make 2)

With 5 mm (US 8) needles cast on 22 (24:26) sts.

Beg with a k row work 21 (23:25) rows in st st, ending with a k row.

Front

With 4½ mm (US 7) needles cast on 96 (100:104) sts.

K 7 rows.

Change to 5 mm (US 8) needles.

Beg with a k row, work 18 (20:22) rows in st st, ending with a p row.

Place pocket

Next row: K13 sts, k next 22 (24:26) sts and leave these sts on a holder, k26 (28:30) sts, k next 22 (24:26) sts and leave these sts on a holder, k last 13 sts.

Next row: P13 sts, p across 22 (24:26) sts of one pocket lining, p26 (28:30), p across 22 (24:26) sts of second pocket lining, p13 sts.

Cont in st st until front measures 44 (46:48) cm (17¼ (18:19) in) from cast-on edge, ending with a p row.

Shape neck

Next row: K38 (40:42), turn and work on these sts for first side of neck shaping.

Dec one st at neck edge on every row until 33 (35:37) sts rem.

Cont straight until front measures the same as back to shoulder, ending at side edge.

Shape shoulder

Cast off.

With right side facing, slip centre 20 sts on to a holder, rejoin yarn to rem sts, k to end.

Complete to match first side.

Sleeves

With 4½ mm (US 7) needles, cast on 36 (38:40) sts.

K 7 rows.

Change to 5 mm (US 8) needles.

Beg with a k row, cont in st st.

Work 4 rows.

Next row (inc row): K3, m1, k to last 3 sts, m1, k3.

Work 5 rows.

Rep the last 6 rows until there are 70 (74:78) sts.

Work straight until sleeve measures 46 (46:48) cm (18 (18:19) in) from cast-on edge, ending with a p row.

Cast off.

Pocket tops

With 4½ mm (US 7) needles, and right side facing, slip sts from pocket front on to a needle.

K 3 rows.

Cast off.

Neckband

Join right shoulder seam.

With 4½ mm (US 7) needles, and right side facing, pick up and k15 sts down left side of front neck, k across 20 sts from front neck holder, pick up and k15 sts up right side of front neck, k across 30 sts from back neck holder. 80 sts.

K 13 rows.

Cast off.

To Make Up

Join left shoulder and neckband seam. With centre of sleeve to shoulder seam, sew on sleeves. Using the invisible seam method (see page 44), join side and sleeve seams. Sew down pocket linings and pocket tops.

Suppliers

UK

Bobbins
Wesley Hall
Church Street
Whitby
North Yorkshire YO22 4DE
Tel/Fax: (01947) 600585
E-mail: bobbins@globalnet.co.uk
Mail order available

Colourway
112A Westbourne Grove
Chepstow Road
London W2 5RU
Tel/Fax: (020) 7229 1432
Mail order available

David Morgan Ltd
26 The Hayes
Cardiff
Wales CF10 1UG
Tel: (029) 2022 1011

Designer Yarns Ltd
Units 8-10 Newbridge Industrial Estate
Pitt Street,
Keighley
West Yorkshire BD21 4PQ
Tel: (01535) 664222
E-mail: lauren@designeryarns.uk.com

Jaeger Handknits
Green Lane Mill
Holmfirth
West Yorkshire HD9 2DX
Tel: (01484) 680050

Liberty plc
214 Regent Street
London W1R 6AH
Tel: (020) 7734 1234
Mail order available

Rowan
102 Gloucester Green
Oxford OX1 2DF
Tel: (01865) 793366
Mail order available

Rowan Yarns
Green Lane Mill
Holmfirth
West Yorkshire HD9 2 DX
Tel: (01484) 681881
Fax: (01484) 687920
Website: www.rowanyarns.co.uk
Worldwide distribution. Phone for details of your nearest stockist

Shoreham Knitting & Needlecraft
19 East Street
Shoreham-by-Sea
West Sussex BN43 5ZE
Tel: (01273) 461029
Fax: (01273) 465407
E-mail: skn@sure-employ.demon.co.uk
Website: www.englishyarns.co.uk
Mail order available

Stitch Shop
15 The Podium
Northgate
Bath BA1 5AL
Tel: (01225) 481134
Mail order available

SOUTH AFRICA

Arthur Bales
62, 4th Avenue
Linden
Johannesburg 2195
Tel: (011) 888 2401

ABC Knitting & Haberdashery
327 President Street
Germiston 1401
Tel: (011) 873 4296

Trienies
Shop 41, Sanlam Centre
Leraatsfontein
Witbank 1034
Tel: (013) 692 4196

The Image
23 Lynwood Shopping Centre
Lynwood Road
Lynwood Ridge
Pretoria 0081
Tel: (012) 361 1737

Knitting Nook
5 Library Lane
Somerset West
Cape Town 7130
Tel: (021) 852 3044
Retail and mail order

Knitting Wool Centre (Pty) Ltd
122 Victoria Road
Woodstock
Cape Town 7925
Tel: (021) 447 1134

Orion Wool Shop and Needlecraft
39 Adderley Street
Cape Town 8000
Tel: (021) 461 6941
Retail and mail order

Little Angel
Shop 4, Newton Spar Centre
3rd Avenue
Newton Park
Port Elizabeth 6045
Tel: (041) 363 9943

Swansdown Knitting Wools (Pty) Ltd
8 Foundry Lane
Durban 4001
Tel: (031) 304 0488

AUSTRALIA

Greta's Handcraft Centre
321 Pacific Highway
LINDFIELD
NSW 2070
Tel: (02) 9416 2489

Jo Sharp Pty Ltd
P.O.Box 357
Albany, WA 6331
Tel: (08) 9842 2250
Website: www.josharp.com.au

Knitters of Australia
498 Hampton Street
HAMPTON
VIC 3188
Tel: (03) 9533 1233

Lindcraft
Gallery Level
Imperial Arcade
Pitt Street
SYDNEY
NSW 2000
Tel: (02) 9221 5111

Sunspun
185 Canterbury Rd
Canterbury
VIC 3126
Tel: (03) 9830 1609

NEW ZEALAND

Knit World
Selected branches stock Rowan wools,
phone first to find out
Branches nationwide:
Auckland – (09) 837 6111
Tauranga – (07) 577 0797
Hastings – (06) 878 0090
New Plymouth – (06) 758 3171
Palmerston North – (06) 356 8974
Wellington – (04) 385 1918
Christchurch – (03) 379 2300
Dunedin – (03) 477 0400

Spotlight
Branches throughout New Zealand
19 Link Drive
Glenfield
Tel: (09) 444 0220
Website: www.spotlightonline.co.nz

Woolmart Wools
Branches throughout South Island and
Auckland
Check listings in your local White or
Yellow Pages (under "Knitting Wool")

USA

Knitting Fever Inc
35 Debevoise Avenue
Roosevelt
New York 11575
Tel: (516) 546 3600
Website: www.knittingfever.com

Rowan USA
4 Townsend West
Nashua
New Hampshire 03063
Tel: (603) 886 5041/5043
E-mail: wfibers@aol.com

CANADA

Diamond Yarns Ltd
155 Martin Ross Avenue
Unit 3, Toronto
Ontario M3J 2L9.
Tel: (416) 736 6111
Website: www.diamondyarn.com

JAPAN

Eisaku Noro & Co Ltd
55 Shimoda Ohibino Azaichou
Ichinomita Aichi, 491 0105
Tel: (81) 52 203 5100

GERMANY

Designer Yarns
Handelsagentur Klaus Koch
Pontinusweg 7, D-50859 Köln,
Tel/Fax: (49) 0234 77573
Website: www.designer-yarns.de

FRANCE

Elle Tricote
8 Rue de Coq
67000 Strasbourg
Tel: (03) 88 23 03 13
Website: www.elletricote.com

BELGIUM

Pavan
Koningin Astridlaan 78,
B9000 Gent
Tel: (32) 9221 8594
E-mail: pavan@pandora.be

Index

Acknowledgments

First and foremost, I would like to thank my mother who taught me to knit when I was five years old, so I could knit all the sleeves for my sisters' jumpers.

Thanks also to Rosemary Wilkinson, who invited me to write this book, Clare Sayer who patiently guided me through the all various stages of editing and book production, Shona Wood for her photography and lunches and Debbie Bliss, Jaeger Handknits and Rowan Yarns for their beautiful yarns. I must also thank the knitters: Dorothy Bayley, Cynthia Brent, Pat Church, Jacqui Dunt, Shirley Kennet and Beryl Salter and Tricia McKenzie for checking all the patterns.

Finally, I'd like to thank my family, who didn't complain too much about the house being full of knitting yarn.